CONTENTS

1   INTRODUCTION

This new edition of the Directory replaces the 1993 edition. In the intervening two years there has been a considerable number of new pieces of legislation. Additionally the subject matter has been extended to cover procurement and associated topics.

The section on Standards and Codes of Practice has been discontinued and only the more pertinent Standards and Codes of Practice are listed. They can be found in the same place in the Directory as the legislation to which they pertain.

Another change is that, in general, amendments to the Regulations are not listed separately but are found in the text for the amended legislation. The exceptions depend on the extent of the amendment.

The most obvious change though, is the change of format to accommodate, (this has been forced by the necessity to facilitate) updates to the Directory. It is felt that the Directory may also be easier to use as a result.

The purpose of this Directory is to list the UK legislation which should be considered when designing, installing and operating building services. This is taken to cover air conditioning, heating, ventilating, plumbing, controls, lighting, power, security, fire protection, lifts, insulation, acoustics, energy and alternative energy. The subject area is wide and the identification of all relevant Regulations and Acts difficult to achieve. However, the Directory contains the important legislation.

DISCLAIMER

(1)   The Directory may not be comprehensive

(2)   Interpretations have no legal standing

---

2   USING THE DIRECTORY

2.1   SUBJECT INDEX

The subject index (Section 8) is the special feature of this Directory. All the Acts and Regulations are indexed uniformly. Under each index term is listed the Acts or Regulations together with the page number which are concerned with this subject. Thus under the subject 'boilers' are listed the Acts and Regulations concerned with boilers. This acts as an aide memoire on legislation which may be necessary to consider if you are installing a boiler. You can then go to the resumés to find out more details. It must be kept in mind that it is the actual legislation and how it is interpreted in the courts of law which is of paramount importance.

2.2   ACTS

Section 5 consists of the Acts of Parliament. For each Act, its commencement date or dates, the part of the UK in which it applies, a brief resume, authorities for enforcement, and Regulations enacted under the Act, are given.

It should be noted that the United Kingdom comprises England, Wales, Scotland and Northern Ireland.

2.3   REGULATIONS

Regulations are published as Statutory Instruments (SI) eg the Building Regulations 1985 are SI 1985/1065, where 1065 represents their position in that year's legislative programme.

Section 6 lists the Regulations in alphabetical order, each one with the date of commencement and the Act under which it was passed, a brief description and a list of the cited British Standards which are considered relevant to building services. Also listed are any other technical documents mentioned in the Regulations. This does not apply to Regulations, like the Building Regulations 1991, which cite numerous British Standards.

Regulations in general contain more technical details than the Acts. Thus, Regulations can be regarded as an index to the Act under which they were made.

2.4   FURTHER INFORMATION

Section 7 lists some explanatory documents and guidance. It also refers to sources of information on legal matters and laws and regulations as they come into force. It also gives sources of information about European law which will increasingly affect the UK.

                                                    ©BSRIA

3   LAW, STANDARDS, INTERPRETATION AND ENFORCEMENT

3.1   THE LEGISLATIVE PROCESS

The primary legislation in the UK is the Act of Parliament. Acts of Parliament can be very specific, but in recent times they have included provision for Regulations or Orders to be made within the framework of the Act. For instance Part 1 of the Building Act 1984 gives the Secretary of State power to make Building Regulations for certain prescribed purposes within certain limitations. Thus we have the Building Regulations 1991 made under this Act as a Statutory Instrument (SI).

Regulations have the same force of law as Acts but are limited by the Act under which they were enacted. For instance the Building Act 1984 does not allow Building Regulations to apply to a school or other educational establishment erected according to plans approved by the Secretary of State for Education. The Building Regulations 1991 do not state this, but it remains an overriding limitation.

The date of the legislation is very important as it is quite possible for later legislation to change earlier Acts. The Health and Safety at Work etc Act 1974 has provision for making Building Regulations. This provision was removed by the Building Act 1984.

In some cases an Act can "take over" earlier regulations. For instance the Cinema Act 1985 consolidated the Cinematograph Acts of 1909 and 1952 and in doing so maintained some regulations made under these previous Acts. In another case, the health and safety regulations made under the Factory Act 1961 were taken over by the Health and Safety at Work etc Act 1974, so that many factory regulations became the responsibility of the Health and Safety Executive.

3.2   STATUS OF STANDARDS AND CODES OF PRACTICE

Regulations often refer to British Standards or Codes of Practice as providing a way of conforming with the Regulations. Sometimes the version of the British Standard referred to has been superseded by later versions or has been withdrawn or is obsolete. This might pose problems but usually conformity with a revised Standard also meets the requirements of the Regulations.

However, other appropriate National Standards, Codes of Practice and Guides not specifically mentioned in legislation should not be ignored. For example, the Health and Safety Executive published detailed guidelines which could form the basis of a prosecution under the Health and Safety at Work etc Act 1974 and also lead to civil action by the public, if an outbreak of legionnaires' disease occurred.

3.3   AUTHORITIES

An authority is usually listed for Acts and Regulations and this authority is responsible for enforcement of the law. This authority can also advise and give an interpretation of the Act or Regulation. An appeal is possible to the Secretary of State or his office. The final decision lies with the Courts of Law. In fact, for many Acts of Parliament there is a record of case law which can be consulted.

In the case of Building Regulations, for example, the first authority is the Building Control Officer of the Local Authority or the Fire Officer if the problem concerns fire precautions. If this local help does not or cannot give an answer which is helpful, the next contact is the Building Regulations section of the Department of the Environment. If their interpretation is not accepted then it is possible to appeal to the Secretary of State for the Environment. The final resort is to the Courts of Law.

©BSRIA

4 EUROPEAN LAW

Council Regulations come into force in the UK as soon as they are published in the Official Journal. This is only possible because the governments concerned are already agreed on the matter. Only one such Regulation is listed in this Directory "Substances that deplete the ozone layer" EEC 595/91. This became effective throughout the European Union (EU) as soon as it was published in the Official Journal on the 4th March 1991.

Council Directives on the other hand, come into force in the UK only after appropriate changes to UK legislation. The changes can be in the form of amendments to existing Regulations or new Regulations. For example, the Workplace Directive resulted in a number of UK Regulations made under the Health & Safety at Work etc Act 1974. There is always a period for consultation with affected groups before such Regulations are passed through Parliament.

BSRIA maintains a database and produces a series of publications on developments in European legislation and standards which affect the building services industry. The Commission of the European Communities has set up a nationwide network of relays in the UK for provision of EU information. For small businesses, there are Euro Information Centres, and for academic institutions and students, European Documentation Centres.

5   ACTS OF PARLIAMENT

5.1   LIST OF ACTS

(ALPHABETICAL ORDER)

5.2   RESUME OF ACTS

Ancient Monuments and Archaeological Areas Act 1979

Commencement: Between 16 July 1979 to 14 April 1982

Applies to England, Wales and Scotland.

To consolidate and amend the law relating to ancient monuments and to make provision for the investigation, preservation and recording of matters of archaeological or historical interest.

Such buildings and sites are excluded from the application of the Building Regulations 1991.

Animals (Scientific Procedures) Act 1986

Commencement: 1st January 1987; its provisions are progressively being brought into force

Applies to England, Wales, Scotland and to Northern Ireland with some modifications.

This Act regulates any experimental or other scientific procedure applied to an animal which may have the effect of causing the animal pain, suffering, distress or lasting harm. Under the Act inspectors have been appointed to visit establishments and an Animal Procedures Committee has been appointed. This Act has been amended by SI 1993/2103 (1/10/93)

Codes of Practice

Code of Practice for the housing and care of animals used in scientific procedures, Home Office, HMSO 1989.

Code of Practice for the housing and care of animals in designated breeding and supplying establishments, Home Office, HMSO 1995.

Building (Scotland) Acts 1959 and 1970

Commencement: 30 April 1959 and 29 May 1970 respectively

Applies to Scotland

These Acts make provision for safety, health and other matters in respect of the construction of buildings and for safety in respect of the conduct of building operations in Scotland. They establish building authorities and amend the powers of local authorities in relation to buildings which are below-standard or dangerous. They give powers to the Secretary of State to make building regulations. The Acts override local Acts.

Authorities   (1)   Local Authorities

                         (2)   Secretary of State

Regulations

Building Standards (Scotland) Regulations 1990 *(Page 46)*

Building Act 1984

Commencement: 31 October 1984

Applies to England and Wales

This is an Act to consolidate certain enactments concerning building and buildings and related matters. It gives the Secretary of State power to make building regulations and abolishes this power under the Health and Safety at Work etc Act 1974. Some regulations can be applied to existing buildings.

Exclusions   (i)   Particular classes of building

                        (ii)   Educational buildings and buildings of statutory undertakers eg British Airports Authority, UK Atomic Energy Authority

                        (iii)   Local authorities or councils

Authorities   (1)   Secretary of State, Secretary of State for Wales

                        (2)   Delegated powers eg to local authorities

                        (3)   Fire Authorities

Regulations

Building (Inner London) Regulations 1985 *(Page 42)*

Building Regulations 1991 *(Page 43)*

Celluloid and Cinematograph Film Act 1922

Commencement: 1st October 1922

Applies to England, Wales, Scotland and Northern Ireland.

An Act to make better provision for the prevention of fire in premises where raw celluloid or cinematograph film is stored.

Authorities   (1)   Local Authority

                         (2)   Fire Authority

Regulations

Cinematograph films, use of apparatus, safety provisions order 1924.
SR & O 1924/403. *(Page 49)*

Cinema Act 1985

Commencement: 27th June 1985

Applies to England, Wales and Scotland.

The Act consolidates the Cinematograph Acts of 1909 to 1982. It is concerned with safety in connection with the giving of film exhibitions (including the keeping and handling of the film material and related equipment). It is also concerned with the health and welfare of children attending the film exhibition.

Section 4 allows regulations to be made. To date one regulation has been made to change the cinema license fee (SI 1991/2462). Some previous regulations have been maintained.

Authorities   (1)   Licensing Authority (Local Authority)

                         (2)   Fire Authorities

                         (3)   Chief Officer of Police

Regulations

Cinematograph (Safety) Regulations 1955/1129 *(Page 49)*. Amended by SI 1958/1530, SI 1965/282, SI 1976/1315, SI 1982/1856.

Clean Air Act 1993

Commencement: 27 August 1993

Applies to England, Wales and Scotland and parts have application in the Scilly Isles and Northern Ireland.

An Act to consolidate the Clean Air Acts of 1958 and 1968 (ie it replaces these Acts). It also amends other Acts such as the Control of Pollution Act 1974, the Local Government Planning and Land Act 1980, the Building Act 1984 and the Environmental Protection Act 1990, plus it repeals the Control of Smoke Pollution Act 1989.

The Act is concerned with the emission of dark smoke, grit dust and fumes from chimneys and furnaces, and the establishment of control zones. It also control of other forms of air pollution relating to motor fuel and the content of fuel oil.

Authorities   (1)   Local Authorities and in default the Secretary of State

Regulations

Health and Safety (Emissions into the Atmosphere) Regulations 1983.
SI 1983/943. *(Page 72)*

Consumer Protection Act 1987

Commencement: After 15th May 1987

Applies to England, Wales and Scotland, and to Northern Ireland (except for Part I Product Liability and Part II Misleading Price Indications).

Concerns liability of persons for damage caused by defective products. It also consolidates with amendments the Consumer Safety Act 1978 *(Page 12)* and the Consumer Safety (amendment) Act 1986. It makes provision for the giving of price indications. It amends Part 1 of the Health and Safety at Work etc Act 1974 and sections 31 and 80 of the Explosives Act 1875. It repeals the Trade Descriptions Act 1972 and the Fabrics (Misdescription) Act 1913.

It puts into UK law a Directive of the Council of the European Communities 5/7/85 (85/374/EEC).

This is a very general Act which makes most persons concerned with production and supply of a product which is defective or unsafe liable to prosecution.

Authorities   (1)   Weights and Measures Authority

              (2)   District Council in Northern Ireland

              (3)   Police Authorities

              (4)   Customs and Excise

Regulations

Approval of Safety Standard Regulations 1987. SI 1987/1911. *(Page 39)*

Asbestos (Safety) Regulations 1985. SI 1985/2042. *(Page 40)*

Electrical Equipment (Safety) Regulations 1994. *(Page 58)*

Gas Appliances (Safety) Regulations 1992. SI 1992/711. *(Page 69)*

Gas Cooking Appliances (Safety) Regulations 1989. SI 1989/149. *(Page 70)*

Low Voltage Electrical Equipment (Safety) Regulations 1989. SI 1989/728. *(Page 75)*

Oil Heaters (Safety) Regulations 1977. SI 1977/167. *(Page 82)*

Consumer Safety Act 1978

Commencement: 20th July 1978

Applies to England, Wales and Scotland, and to Northern Ireland with some modifications.

This Act makes further provision with regard to the safety of consumers and others. It allows the Secretary of State to issue prohibition orders on unsafe products.

Authorities   (1)   Weights and Measures Authorities

                  (2)   Secretary of State

Control of Pollution Act 1974

Commencement: Various sections came into force from 1st January 1974. To some degree superseded by the Environmental Protection Act 1991

Applies to England, Wales and Scotland but not Northern Ireland except for five sections.

The Act is concerned with waste disposal, pollution of water, and noise pollution.

Authorities   (1)   Disposal Authorities

                         (2)   Water Authority

Regulations

Control of Noise (Code of Practice for Construction Sites) Order 1975.
SI 1975/2115. *(Page 55)*

Control of Noise (Code of Practice on Noise from Audible Intruder Alarms) Order 1981. SI 1981/1829. *(Page 55)*

Oil Fuel (Sulphur Content of Gas Oil) Regulations SI 1976/1988. *(Page 82)*

For fuller list see Halsbury's Statutes 4th Ed. 1987, Vol.35, Public Health pp17-18, Butterworth, 1987.

Control of Pollution (Amendment) Act 1989

Commencement: 6th July 1989

Applies to England, Wales and Scotland.

Provides for the registration of carriers of controlled waste and for making further provision with respect to the powers exercisable in relation to vehicles shown to have been used for illegal waste disposal.

Education Acts 1944-1985

Commencement: After 3rd August 1944

Applies to England and Wales.

This is an Act to reform the law relating to education in England and Wales. It deals with standards for education premises and allows for regulations to be made.

School buildings erected according to plans of the Secretary of State for Education and Science [and for Wales] are exempt from part 1 of the Building Act and therefore from all regulations made under the Act.

Authorities   (1)   Department for Education

                         (2)   Local Authorities

Regulations

Education (School Premises) Regulations 1981. SI 1981/909. *(Page 57)*

Electricity Act 1989

Commencement: After 1st April 1989

Applies to England, Wales and Scotland.

The Act established the Privatised Electricity Companies and their functions and replaces previous Electricity Acts.

Authorities   (1)   Electricity Companies

                         (2)   Electricity Association

Energy Act 1983

Commencement: In part 1st June 1983 and 1st September 1983

Applies to England, Wales and Scotland and in Northern Ireland except for some parts.

An Act to amend the law relating to electricity so as to facilitate the generation and supply of electricity by persons other than Electricity Boards, and to amend the law relating to duties of persons responsible for nuclear installations and to compensate for breach of those duties.

Regulations

Electricity (Private Generating Stations and Requests by Private Generators and Suppliers) Regulation 1984. SI 1984/136. *(Not listed in this issue of the Directory)*

Fuel and Electricity (Heating) (Control) (Amendment) Order 1980. SI 1980/1013. *(Page 68)*

Environmental Protection Act 1990

Commencement: Part on 1st January 1991 and as ordered by the Secretary of State

Applies to England and Wales.

The Act established the concept of integrated pollution control, where emissions are controlled whether they are to air, land or water. A new inspectorate, Her Majesty's Inspectorate of Pollution (HMIP) has been created which combines three existing inspectorates, industrial air pollution, radioactive substances and hazardous waste, within it. This is also an enabling Act which allows Regulations to be passed under it.

Guidance

The Secretary of State has published Process Guidance Notes for specified processes eg clinical waste incineration, crematoria, large boilers and furnaces. Available from HMSO.

Regulations

Controlled Waste (Registration of Carriers and Seizure of Vehicles) Regulations 1991. SI 1991/1624. *(Page 56)*

Environmental Protection (Applications, Appeals and Registers) Regulations 1991. SI 1991/507. *(Page 61)*

Environmental Protection (Authorisation of Processes) (Determination of Periods) Order 1991. SI 1991/513. *(Page 61)*

Environmental Protection (Controls of Injurious Substances) Regulations 1992. SI 1992/31. *(Page 61)*

Environmental Protection (Determination of Enforcing Authority etc.) (Scotland) Regulations 1992. SI 1992/530. *(Page 62)*

Environmental Protection (Duty of Care) Regulations 1991. SI 1991/2839. *(Page 62)*

Environmental Protection (Proscribed Processes and Substances) Regulations 1991. SI 1991/472. *(Page 63)*

Environmental Protection (Proscribed Processes and Substances) (Amendment) Regulations 1992. SI 1992/614. *(Page 63)*

European Communities Act 1972

Commencement: 17th October 1972

Applies to England, Wales, Scotland and Northern Ireland, and for some purposes to the Channel Islands, the Isle of Man and Gibraltar.

An Act to make provision in connection with the enlargement of the European Communities to include the UK. It allows the Directives of the European Commission to be translated into UK law.

Regulations

Air Quality Standards Regulations. SI 1989/317. *(Page 39)*

Construction Products Regulations. SI 1991/1620. *(Page 52)*

Electrically, Hydraulically and Oil-Electrically Operated Lifts (Components) (EEC Requirements) Regulations 1991. SI 1991/2748. *(Page 58)*

Gas Appliances (Safety) Regulations. SI 1992/711. *(Page 69)*

Measuring Instruments (EEC Requirements) (Electrical Energy Meters) Regulations. SI 1980/886. *(Page 77)*

Measuring Instruments (EEC Requirements) (Gas Volume Meters) Regulations. SI 1983/1246. *(Page 77)*

Safety Signs Regulations 1980. SI 1980/1471. *(Page 89)*

Substances which deplete the ozone layer.

Plus many others too numerous to be listed.

Explosive Substances Act 1875 and Explosives Act 1923

Commencement: 14th June 1875 and 18th July 1923

Applies to England, Wales, Scotland and Northern Ireland.

An Act to amend the law with respect to manufacturing, storing, selling, transporting and importing gunpowder, nitro-glycerine and other explosive substances.

Authorities   (1)   Health and Safety Executive

                         (2)   Inspectors

Regulations

Many regulations have been made under these Acts.

For a listing see Halsbury's Statutes 4th Ed. Vol.17, pp24-26, Butterworth, 1987.

Factories Act 1961

Commencement: 1st April 1962

Applies to England, Wales and Scotland.

The Act relates to the safety, health and welfare of employed persons. When the Health and Safety at Work etc Act 1974 came into force it took over many aspects of this Act by repealing part of it through The Factories Act 1961 (repeals) Regulations 1975.

The definition of a factory is any premises where work is taking place employing two or more persons even in the open air, but excludes premises covered by the Office, Shops and Railway Premises Act 1963.

Authorities

There are many authorities involved for various aspects of the Act:

(1)	District Councils
(2)	Medical Officer of Health
(3)	Factory Inspector
(4)	Competent Person
(5)	Fire Authority
(6)	Local Authority
(7)	Health and Safety Executive
(8)	Minister of Employment

Regulations

Numerous regulations have been made under this Act. For listing see Halsbury's Statutes 4th Ed.1987 Vol.19, pp15-20, Butterworth, 1987.

All Regulations made under this Act concerned with health and safety have been transferred to the Health and Safety Executive.

Fire Precautions Act 1971

Commencement: 27th May 1971

Applies to England, Wales and Scotland but not Northern Ireland except for two sections.

Act to protect persons from fire risks in premises not covered by other Acts.

Authorities   (1)   Fire Authority

                         (2)   Local Authority

Guidance

The Home Office has issued guides to the fire precautions required under this Act in various types of premises which require a fire certificate. These include existing places of work, hotels, and boarding houses. Available from HMSO.

Regulations

Fire Precautions (Application for a Certificate) Regulations 1989. SI 1989/77. *(Page 64)*

Fire Precautions (Factories, Offices, Shops and Railway Premises) Order 1989. SI 1989/76. *(Page 64)*

Fire Precautions (Hotels and Boarding Houses) Order 1972. SI 1972/238. *(Page 65)*

Fire Precautions (Sub-Surface Railway Stations) Regulations 1989. SI 1989/1401. *(Page 66)*

Fire Safety and Safety of Places of Sport Act 1987

Commencement: 15th May 1987 and in stages. The last commencement order found being in force on 31st December 1990.

Applies to England, Scotland and Wales but not Northern Ireland.

An Act to amend the Fire Precautions Act 1971 and other enactments relating to Fire Precautions; to amend the Safety of Sports Grounds Act 1975 and to make like provision for sports premises. It provides for the licensing of indoor sports premises outside London.

Fire Services Act 1947

Commencement: 31st July 1947

Applies to England, Wales and Scotland.

This Act made County Councils responsible for their local fire services. One of the duties of the fire service is to give, when requested, advice in respect of buildings and other property in their area as to fire prevention, restricting the spread of fires and means of escape in case of fire.

Food Safety Act 1990

Commencement: 1st January 1991, but application to Crown Premises dates from 1st April 1992.

Applies to England, Wales, Scotland.

The Food Safety Act 1990 replaces most of the provisions of the Food Act 1984. It redefines "Food" and now applies to all stages of the food chain. Its principal aims are to:-

(a)   assure that all food produced for human consumption is safe to eat and not misleadingly presented

(b)   strengthen enforcement powers and increase penalties

(c)   harmonise UK laws and standards with those of the rest of Europe

(d)   take into account technological changes

The Act allows for regulations to be passed to implement requirements. It maintains in force the Food Hygiene (General) Regulations 1970, and two recent amendments have been enacted: the Food Hygiene (Amendment) Regulations of 1990 and 1991. *(Page 66)*.

Authorities   (1)   Food Authority = Local Authority

(2)   Customs & Excise

(3)   Public Health Authority

Regulations

Regulations passed under this Act begin with the word 'Food' so are easily identifiable. *(Pages 66, 67)*

Gas Act 1986

Commencement: 23rd July 1986

Applies to England, Wales and Scotland.

The aim of this Act is to facilitate the privatisation of gas supplies. It sets up a Director General of Gas supplies and a Gas Consumers' Council. It removes the privileged position of the British Gas Corporation and then abolishes it to be replaced by British Gas plc.

Authorities   (1)   Secretary of State

                        (2)   British Gas

Regulations

Gas (Meters) Regulations 1983. SI 1983/684. *(Page 68)*

Gas Catalytic Heaters (Safety Requirements) Sales of Goods. SI 1984/1802. *(Page 69)*

Gas Safety (Installation and Use) Regulations 1994. SI 1994/1886. *(Page 70)*

Gas Safety Regulations 1972. SI 1972/1178. *(Page 71)*

Health and Safety at Work etc Act 1974

Commencement: Various dates after 31 July 1974

Applies to England, Wales, Scotland except for most of Part III; Not to Northern Ireland except part of Part I. Applies also off-shore due to an Act of Parliament the Off-shore Safety Act 1992. *(Page 24)*.

This Act is concerned with health, safety and welfare in connection with work and the control of dangerous substances and certain emissions to the atmosphere. Its main innovation was to make everyone at a workplace have responsibility for safety and also have responsibility for other persons eg visitors who may be injured by factory activities.

Authorities   (1)   Health and Safety Executive/Commission

                        (2)   Secretary of State

                        (3)   Inspectors

Cited Standards

Approved Codes of Practice including, for example IEE Wiring Regulations (BS 7671:1992).

From time to time the Health and Safety Executive has issued Codes of Practice. After these are issued it is possible that non-compliance and a complaint can together bring legal action.

Regulations

All Regulations concerned with Health and Safety in Workplaces are made under this Act but are too numerous to list here.

Housing Act 1980

Commencement: 8th August 1980. Some parts came into force immediately, others eight weeks later. It is not all in force yet.

Applies to England and Wales. Some parts apply to Scotland and Northern Ireland.

The main aim of the Act is to give security of tenure and the right to buy to tenants of Local Authorities and other bodies. Its main concern for building services is the means of escape in case of fire. Some parts have been repealed.

Authorities   (1)   Housing Authority (and Fire Authority)

Regulations

Housing (Means of Escape From Fire in Houses in Multiple Occupation) Order 1981. SI 1981/1576. *(Page 73)*

Local Acts

Building control in the UK has been exercised by local government since the 12th Century. London, for instance, has its own local act London Building Acts (Amendment) Act 1939, *(Page 22)* but so do about 30 other local authorities. Local bye-laws are made under powers granted by these Acts or under the various local government Acts but they cannot conflict with Building Regulations made under the Building Act 1984.

Subjects covered, of interest to building services, are flammable substances, fire precautions, firemen's switches, means of escape, oil-burning equipment, dust, hazard signs and temporary structures.

London

The Greater London Council (GLC) was abolished by the Local Government (Miscellaneous Provisions) (no.4) Order 1986.

This order, made under the Local Government Act 1985, came into operation on 1st April 1986. It transferred building control powers from the GLC to the Inner London Borough Councils. It made the Fire and Civil Defence Authority the "Fire Authority for Greater London".

The GLC bye-laws are in general still in force, but administered by each London Borough.

Scotland

Only the main Act, Building (Scotland) Acts 1959 and 1970 *(Page 8)* and the Regulations, Building Standards (Scotland) Regulations 1990. *(Page 46)* made under it are considered with regard to Scotland.

London Building Acts (Amendment) Act 1939

Commencement: 1st January 1940

This is a local act for inner London (see also Local Acts, *page 21)*. It covers all types of building and buildings including taller or larger buildings. Particular buildings are excluded from the Building Regulations, such as the Bank of England, Covent Garden etc. The list of exclusions is large and also includes Crown property.

Nevertheless, excluded buildings can come under regulations due to licensing for other use eg, The Albert Hall as a concert hall. The Health and Safety at Work Act 1974 may also apply for those working in these buildings.

Some parts of this Act have been repealed by the Building (Inner London) Regulations 1985 *(Page 42)* eg sections 16-18 and sections 22-28. This Act was also modified by these Regulations, in particular the first two subsections of section 20 concerned with large or tall buildings. This section has been clarified and some requirements given more detail eg adequate ventilation for a fire risk area is defined.

Section 21 has been amended by the Building (Inner London) Regulations 1987.

Authorities   (1)   Local Authorities

                          (2)   Fire and Civil Defence Authority

Cited Standards

Electrical Regulations of the Institution of Electrical Engineers (BS 7671:1992).

Mines and Quarries Act 1954

Commencement: 25th November 1954

Applies to England, Wales and Scotland.

Concerns the management and control of mines and quarries and the health, safety and welfare of persons employed in them.

Authorities   (1)   Trade Unions

(2)   Health and Safety Executive

(3)   Secretary of State

Regulations

A considerable number of Statutory Instruments have been made under this Act but are not considered relevant to building services.

For more details see Halsbury's Statutes 4th Ed. 1987, Vol 29, pp18, 19, Butterworth, 1987.

Occupiers' Liability Acts 1957 and 1984

Commencement: 1957 Act, 1st January 1958; 1984 Act, 13th May 1984

Applies to England and Wales.

The 1957 Act concerns the liability of occupiers and others for injury and damage resulting to persons or goods lawfully on any land or other property from dangers due to the state of the property or to things done or omitted to be done there.

The 1984 Act concerns the same liability but for persons other than visitors. It amends the Unfair Contract Terms Act 1977, in relation to persons obtaining access to premises for recreational or educational purposes. It protects people who enter premises without invitation or permission eg trespassers but equally, persons who enter by lawful authority eg through a private right of way.

The scope of these Acts has been and is established by case law.

Off-shore Safety Act 1992

Commencement: 6th March 1992, but not wholly. A commencement order brought parts in force on 30/11/93.

Applies to Offshore England, Wales, Scotland and Northern Ireland.

This Act extends Part I of the Health and Safety at Work etc Act 1974 to include off-shore installations. It also increases the levels of fines available under the 1974 Act.

Authorities   (1)   Health and Safety Executive

Offices, Shops, and Railway Premises Act 1963

Commencement: Various dates

Applies to England, Wales, and Scotland.

Covers offices, shops and railway premises. It deals with safety, working conditions, minimum area per person, fire prevention, fire precautions, fire alarms, fire fighting equipment and fuel storage on these premises.

Authorities   (1)   Local Authorities

(2)   Fire Authorities

(3)   Factory Inspectors

(4)   National Radiological Protection Board

Regulations

Sanitary Conveniences Regulations 1964. SI 1964/966. *(Page 90)*

Washing Facilities Regulations 1964. SI 1964/965. *(Page 93)*

Petroleum (Consolidation) Act 1928

Commencement: 3rd August 1928

Applies to England, Wales and Scotland.

An Act to consolidate the enactments relating to petroleum and petroleum spirit.

Authorities   (1)   Local Authorities

Regulations

Regulations have been made under the Act but they do not appear to be especially relevant to building services.

Planning (Hazardous Substances) Act 1990

Commencement: 24th May 1990

Applies to England and Wales.

Provides for Regulations to be passed to bring it into operation. It requires a hazardous substance consent to be obtained where a controlled quality of a hazardous substance is present on, over, or under land.

Authorities   (1)   The Council of the District

                         (2)   London Borough Council

These are designated as the Hazardous Substances Authorities

Regulations

Planning (Hazardous Substances) Regulations 1992. SI 1992/656. *(Page 84)*

Planning (Listed Buildings and Conservation Areas) Act 1990

Commencement: 24 August 1990

Applies to England and Wales.

An Act to consolidate certain enactments relating to special controls in respect to buildings and areas of special architectural or historic interest. The Secretary of State is empowered to compile or approve the list of such buildings or areas. Work is restricted on such buildings. The list of buildings or areas is published and available for public inspection at convenient places.

Planning and Compensation Act 1991

Commencement: This Act received the Royal Assent on 25th July 1991 and partly came into force on that date, but mainly comes into force by Orders; some 5 Commencement Orders were passed in 1991.

Parts I and III apply to England and Wales only; other parts to Scotland only; it mostly does not apply to Northern Ireland.

It provides for new enforcement powers and for other controls over development. It confers powers to the Historic Buildings and Monuments Commission regarding information required for the Planning (Listed Buildings and Conservation Areas) Act 1990.

Property Misdescription Act 1991

Commencement: Received Royal Assent 27th June but in force 4th April 1993.

Applies to England, Wales, Scotland and Northern Ireland.

The Act makes it an offence to give a false description of property. It is aimed at estate agents and property developers in particular.

Radioactive Substances Act 1993

Commencement:

Applies to England, Wales, Scotland and Northern Ireland.

Consolidates and repeals previous Acts of the same name from 1948 and 1960. Regulates the keeping and use of radioactive substances and the accumulation and disposal of radioactive waste.

Authorities	(1)	Her Majesty's Inspectorate of Pollution (England and Wales)
	(2)	Scottish Office Environment Department
	(3)	Department of the Environment for Northern Ireland

Radiological Protection Act 1970

Commencement: 1st October 1970

Applies to England, Wales, Scotland, and Northern Ireland (with some amendments).

Establishes a National Radiological Protection Board and an advisory committee with functions concerning the protection of people from radiation hazards, and for connected purposes.

Authorities   (1)   National Radiological Protection Board

Registered Homes Act 1984

Commencement: 26th June 1984

Applies to England, Wales and the Isles of Scilly.

Consolidates certain enactments relating to residential care homes, nursing homes and registered homes tribunals.

It covers specifically equipment in the homes, but registration implies consideration of health and safety in these premises.

Authorities   (1)   Registration Authority

                        (2)   Social Services

                        (3)   Local Authorities

                        (4)   Registered Homes Tribunal

                        (5)   Fire Authorities

Regulations

Nursing Homes and Mental Homes Regulations 1984. SI 1984/1578 amended SI 1986/456. *(Page 80)*

Residential Care Homes Regulations 1984. SI 1984/1345 amended SI 1986/457. *(Page 89)*

Safety of Sports Grounds Act 1975

Commencement: 1st September 1974

Applies to England, Wales and Scotland.

The Act makes provision for safety at sports stadia and other sports grounds.

Authorities   (1)   Local Authorities

                          (2)   Fire Authority

                          (3)   Police

                          (4)   Building Authority

Sale of Goods Act 1979

Commencement: 1st January 1980

Applies England, Wales and Northern Ireland, with some special references to Scotland.

The Act consolidates the law relating to the sale of goods. It deals with contracts, the effects of the contract, and the performance of the contract and actions for breach of the contract, and some other related matters.

Regulations

Consumer Protection (Cancellation of Contracts Concluded Away From Business Premises) Regulations 1988. SI 1988/958. *(Page 53)*

Smoke Detectors Act 1991

Commencement: 25th July 1991

Applies to England and Wales.

An Act to make provision for the fitting of smoke detectors in new dwellings. It will be brought in force by order of the Secretary of State at some later date.

Authorities   (1)   Local Authorities

Town and Country Planning (Scotland) Act 1972

Commencement: 27th July 1972

Applies to Scotland.

Consolidates certain enactments relating to town and country planning in Scotland. Establishes a Joint Planning Enquiry Commission to coordinate the law with regard to England and Scotland.

It was amended by the Town and Country Planning (Amendment) Act 1972.

Town and Country Planning Act 1990

Commencement: 24th August 1990

Applies to England and Wales.

An Act to consolidate enactments relating to town and country planning (excluding special controls in respect of buildings and areas of special architectural or historic interest and in respect of hazardous substances). It sets up planning authorities and the final appeal is the Secretary of State. It provides for compensation.

Water Industries Act 1991, Water Resources Act 1991, Land Drainage Act 1991, Statutory Water Companies Act 1991, Water Consolidation (Consequential Provisions) Act 1991

Commencement: 15th July 1991

Apply to England and Wales.

These five Acts together, consolidate the law with regard to water. Under the now-replaced Water Act 1989, the Water Companies were privatised and at the same time two regulatory bodies were set up. The National Rivers Authority looks after water supplies at source. Amongst its responsibilities is the strict regulation of discharges into streams, rivers, and lakes, and into the sea. The other regulatory body is the Office of Water Services (OFWAT) which acts in the customer interests on levels of charge and standards of service.

Authorities   (1)   The Drinking Water Inspectorate

                                    (2)   Her Majesty's Inspectorate of Pollution

Water (Scotland) Act 1980

Commencement: 1st August 1980

This was a consolidation Act for Scotland.

Authorities   (1)   Local Authorities

                       (2)   River Purification Boards

Water law in Northern Ireland is made by a UK Government department.

Authorities   (1)   Department of the Environment for Northern Ireland.
                                *(NB The Government does intend to privatise the
                                water service in NI)*

Wireless Telegraphy Acts 1949 to 1967 and the Telecommunication Act 1984

Commencement: 30 July 1949 to 27 July 1967 and 12 April 1984

Apply to England, Wales, Scotland and Northern Ireland.

These Acts are concerned with control of telecommunications in the UK and with a view to preventing interference.

The Electromagnetic Compatibility Regulations 1992 *(Page 59)* also need to be considered.

Regulations

Wireless Telegraphy (Control of Interference from Handheld Appliances, Portable Tools, etc.) (Amendment) Regulations 1985. SI 1985/808. *(Page 94)*

Wireless Telegraphy (Control of Interference from Ignition Apparatus) Regulations 1973. SI 1973/1217. *(Page 94)*

Wireless Telegraphy (Interference from Citizens' Band Radio) Regulations 1982. SI 1982/635. *(Page 95)*

Wireless Telegraphy (Interference from Electromechanical Apparatus) Regulations 1963. SI1963/189. *(Page 95)*

Wireless Telegraphy (Interference from Fluorescent Lighting Apparatus) (Amendment) Regulations 1985. SI 1985/807. *(Page 95)*

Wireless Telegraphy (Interference from Radio Frequency Heating Apparatus) Regulations 1971. SI 1971/1675. *(Page 96)*

6   REGULATIONS

6.1   LIST OF REGULATIONS

(ALPHABETICAL ORDER)

6.2   LIST OF SI NUMBERS

(DATE/NUMERICAL ORDER)

6.3   RESUME OF REGULATIONS

Air Quality Standards Regulations 1989
SI 1989/317

Commencement: 31st March 1989

Apply to England, Wales, Scotland and Northern Ireland.

Made under the European Communities Act 1972.

These Regulations implement EEC Council Directives 80/779 on air quality limit values and give the value for sulphur dioxide and suspended particulate, 82/884 on limit values for lead in air, 85/203 on air quality standards for nitrogen dioxide.

Animals (Scientific Procedures) Act (Amendment) Regulations 1993
SI 1993/2102

Commencement: 1st October 1993

Apply to England, Wales, Scotland and Northern Ireland.

Made under the European Communities Act 1972.

The 1986 Animals (Scientific Procedures) Act amended so that only in exceptional circumstances can animals belonging to endangered species be used for experimental or other scientific purposes. Implements article 4 of European Council Directive 86/609/EEC.

A further order was made 1993/2103 which added quail to animals which can only be obtained from designated breeding or supplier establishments.

Approval of Safety Standard Regulations 1987
SI 1987/1911

Commencement: 7th December 1987

Apply to England, Wales, Scotland and Northern Ireland.

Made under the Consumer Protection Act 1982.

These Regulations give the Secretary of State the right to approve and disapprove standards of safety. He will give notice of approval or disapproval in the journals "BSI News" and "British Business". A list will also be posted in the library of the Department of Environment.

Asbestos (Licensing) Regulations 1983
SI 1983/1649

Commencement: 1st August 1984

Apply to England, Wales, and Scotland.

Made under the Health & Safety at Work etc Act 1974.

These Regulations require licensing by the HSE of an employer or self-employed person undertaking work with asbestos insulation or asbestos coating. An employer is required to ensure regular medical examination of his employees.

Guidance Note

A Guide to the Asbestos (Licensing) Regulations HS(R)19, HSE, HMSO.

Asbestos (Prohibitions) Regulations 1992
SI 1992/3067

Commencement: 1st January 1993

Apply to England, Wales, and Scotland.

Made under the Health and Safety at Work etc Act 1974.

Implement EEC Directives and replace the 1985 Regulation. Prohibit the import, supply and use of all forms of amphibole asbestos (crocidolite, amosite, fibrous actinolite, fibrous anthophyllite and fibrous tremolite and mixtures containing these).

Asbestos (Safety) Regulations 1985
SI 1985/2042

Commencement: partly 1st January 1986, fully 30th March 1986

Apply to England, Wales, Scotland and Northern Ireland.

Made under the Consumer Protection Act 1987.

Amended by the Asbestos Products (Safety) (Amendment) Regulations 1987
SI 1987/1979

These regulations as amended implement an EEC Directive, 76/769 and amendments. The Regulations prohibit the supply of specific asbestos minerals and products which contain them (with some exceptions).

Batteries and Accumulators (Containing Dangerous Substances) Regulations 1994
SI 1994/232

Commencement: 1st March 1994 (in part) and 1st August 1994

Apply to England, Wales and Scotland.

Made under European Communities Act 1972.

Implement EC Directives 91/157/EEC and 93/86/EEC for controlling release into the environment of lead, mercury and cadmium from batteries. Apply to batteries containing specified quantities of these materials. Prohibit the marketing of high mercury alkaline manganese batteries and require that certain appliances are designed for ease of removal of batteries.

Boiler (Efficiency) Regulations 1993
SI 1993/3083

Commencement: 1st January 1994 except Reg 9 which came into force 1st January 1995

Apply to England, Wales and Scotland

The Regulations define the efficiency requirements for new hot water boilers fired with liquid or gaseous fuels

New boilers will have to meet efficiency standards and will have to bear the CE mark. The Regulations prohibit the supply or putting into service of new boilers which are not up to standard. Amended by SI 1994/3083 (in force 1/1/95) which implements European Directive 92/42 amended by 93/68 on these matters.

Nothing in these Regulations as amended prevents the supply of boilers or appliances which comply with UK rules in force on 21/5/92, until 1st January 1998. These Regulations also do not apply to a back boiler or boiler designed to be installed in a living space so long as the living-space boiler is clearly labelled that this is where it should be installed.

Building (Disabled People) Regulations 1987
SI 1987/1445

Commencement: 14th December 1987

Apply to England, Wales, and Scotland.

Made under the Building Act 1984.

These Regulations were amended and taken over in essence by the Building Regulations 1991 *(Page 43)*

Building (Inner London) Regulations 1985 and 1987
SI 1985/1936, SI 1987/798

Commencement: 6th January 1986 and 1st July 1987 (resp.)

(i)   Apply to Inner London - the area comprising the inner London boroughs, the City of London, the Inner Temple and the Middle Temple;

(ii)   Apply to buildings in conformance with the Building Regulations 1991

These Regulations bring into force for Inner London sections of the Building Act 1984 and the current Building Regulations and other Regulations with minor amendments.

Changes are made to the London Building Acts (Amendment) Act 1939 *(Page 22)*. Some sections are repealed and others are modified. Section 20, which deals with large and high buildings in London, has been modified. Also London bye-laws have been disentangled from the Act. Further modification was made to the Act by Building (Inner London) Regulations 1987 affecting drainage and Section 21 regarding steel doors or roller shutters.

The area of interest of these regulations extends and includes those of the Building Regulations 1991.

Authorities   (1)   Local Authorities

                         (2)   Fire Authorities

                         (3)   Department of the Environment

Building Regulations (Amendment) Regulations 1992
SI 1992/1180

Commencement: 26th June 1992

Apply to England and Wales.

Made under the Building Act 1984.

These Regulations require the deposit with the local authority of two additional sets of plans demonstrating compliance with fire safety requirements, except for a dwelling house or flat.

Building Regulations 1991
SI 1991/2768

Commencement: 1st June 1992

Apply to England and Wales but not inner London.

Made under the Building Act 1984.

Apply to:

(i)   Any building permanent or temporary (but not other kinds of structure or erection), except the following:-

- Buildings controlled by other legislation, eg the Explosives Acts 1875 and 1923; Nuclear Installations Act 1965; Ancient Monuments and Archaeological Areas Act 1979

- Buildings not frequented by people

- Greenhouses and agricultural buildings

- Temporary buildings less than 28 days and mobile homes

- Certain ancillary buildings, eg building site huts

- Small detached buildings of floor area less than 30m^2 which meet other criteria

- Small extensions at ground level eg greenhouse, conservatory, porch, car port

There are 14 Approved Documents associated with these Regulations. These documents contain practical guidance to the requirements of the

Regulations. Some of those approved for the 1985 Regulations are still operative:-

D.   Toxic substances   1985 edition

H.   Drainage and waste disposal   1990 edition

Under the Building Regulations (Amendment) Regulations 1994 SI 1994/1850 two new Approved Documents were issued. *Commencement 1st July 1995.*

F.   Ventilation (1995 edition)

L.   Conservation of fuel and power (1995 edition)

Some new or revised documents have been published as 1992 editions:-

A.   Structure (loading, ground movement, disproportionate collapse)

B.   Fire safety (means of escape, internal fire spread (linings), internal fire spread (structure), external fire spread, access and facilities for the fire services)

C.   Site preparation and resistance to moisture (preparation of site, dangerous and offensive substances (including radon and landfill gas), subsoil drainage, resistance to weather and ground moisture)

E.   Resistance to the passage of sound (airborne sound (walls), airborne sound (floors and stairs), impact sound (floors and stairs))

F.   Ventilation

G.   Hygiene (sanitary conveniences and washing facilities, bathrooms, hot water storage)

J.   Heat producing appliances.

K.   Stairs, ramps and guards (stairs and ramps, protection from falling, vehicle barriers)

L.   Conservation of fuel and power

M.   Access and facilities for disabled people (interpretation, access and use of sanitary conveniences, audience or spectator seating)

N.   Glazing - materials and protection *(NB. This is a new Approved Document, mostly concerned with glazing in passageways)*

REG. 7   Materials and workmanship

Authorities

(1)   Local Authority (Building Control Officer)

(2)   Fire Authority

(3)   British Gas

(4)   Department of the Environment

NB   The crucial requirement is notification to the Local Authority of impending work covered by the Regulations.

Cited Standards etc

There are numerous documents cited in these regulations. Most are cited as being sufficient to conform with the law.

Building Regulations (Northern Ireland) 1990
SI 1990/59

Commencement: 1st June 1990

Apply to Northern Ireland.

Made under the Building Regulations (Northern Ireland) Order 1979.

These Regulations revoke and replace the 1977 Regulations and any amendment made to these Regulations.

Technical booklets were prepared by the Department of the Environment for Northern Ireland which provide guidance which, if followed, ensures compliance with the Regulations as follows:-

C.   Site preparation and resistance to moisture

D.   Structure

G.   Sound

N.   Drainage

These Building Regulations were amended by the Building (Amendment) Regulations (NI) 1991/169 by which two more technical booklets were issued:-

F.   Conservation of fuel and power

L.   Heat-producing appliances

These came into force on 1st July 1991.

Building Regulations (Northern Ireland) 1994. SI 1994/243 brought in two new technical booklets:-

E.   Fire safety (June 1994)

P.   Unvented hot water systems (June 1994)

Authorities   (1)   Local Authorities

                         (2)   Department of the Environment for Northern Ireland

Building Standards (Scotland) Regulations 1990
SI 1990/2179

Commencement: 1st April 1990

Apply to Scotland.

Made under the Building (Scotland) Acts 1959 and 1970

These Regulations replace the 1981 Regulations and amendments. The regulations govern Building Control in Scotland. This includes the construction, alteration, extension or demolition of a building or part of a building or to any change of use which attracts additional or more onerous requirements. The areas covered are:-

Part B:	Fitness of materials
Part C:	Structure
Part D:	Structural fire precautions
Part E:	Means of escape from fire and facilities for fire-fighting
Part F:	Heat-producing installations and storage of liquid and gaseous fuels
Part G:	Preparation of sites and resistance to moisture
Part H:	Resistance to transmission of sound
Part J:	Conservation of fuel and power
Part K:	Ventilation of buildings
Part M:	Drainage and sanitary facilities
Part N:	Electrical installations
Part P:	Miscellaneous hazards
Part Q:	Facilities for dwellings
Part R:	Solid waste storage, dungsteads and farm effluent tanks
Part S:	Stairs, ramps and protective barriers
Part T:	Facilities for disabled people

Part P covers collision with projections, collision with glazing, cleaning of windows, emergency stopping of escalators and passenger conveyers, discharge of steam or hot water, unvented hot water systems.

                                                      ©BSRIA

NB   *A building warrant must be obtained in advance of construction from the local building control authority.*

Authorities   (1)   Local Building Control Authority or if in dispute the Local Authority and still not resolved, Sheriff Court

                            (2)   Fire Authorities

Official Guidance

(a)   Technical Standards. For compliance with the Building Standards (Scotland) Regulations 1990, Edinburgh, HMSO, October 1990

(b)   Small Buildings Guide for compliance with Part C of the Technical Standards, HMSO, 1990

Cited Standards etc

Many Standards are quoted as being deemed-to-satisfy the requirements.

Building Standards (Scotland) Amendment Regulations 1994
SI 1994/1266 (S65)

Commencement: 3oth June 1994

Apply to Scotland.

Made under the Building (Scotland) Act 1959. Amend in various ways the Building Standard (Scotland) Regulations 1990 SI 1990/2179

Regulation 11	Provision for avoiding disproportionate collapse in buildings of five or more storeys
Regulation 25	Changed requirements for sanitary equipment
Regulation 27	Extended safety requirements for roof and window access
Regulation 32	No specific reference to raised floors
Regulation 33	Extended access, aids and facilities for disabled people

The corresponding Technical Standards have also been amended.

Carriage of Dangerous Goods by Rail Regulations 1994
SI 1994/670

Commencement: 1st April 1994

Apply to England, Wales and Scotland.

Made under Health and Safety at Work Act 1974.

Impose requirements and prohibitions with respect to the carriage of dangerous goods by rail in freight containers, packages, tank containers or wagons. All these methods of carriage must be suitable for the purpose, and documentation and labelling provisions must be complied with. Suitable training and information must be provided.

Carriage of Dangerous Goods by Road and Rail (Classification, Packaging and Labelling) Regulations 1994
SI 1994/669

Commencement: 1st April 1994

Apply to England, Wales and Scotland.

Made under Health and Safety at Work Act 1974.

Amend various other Regulations.

Require consignors of dangerous goods being transported by road or rail to ensure they are correctly classified, packaged and labelled. They bring the UK into line with the rest of Europe.

Chemicals (Hazard Information and Packaging for Supply) Regulations 1994
SI 1994/3247

Commencement: 31st January 1995

Apply to England, Wales and Scotland.

Made under the European Communities Act 1972 and the Health and Safety at Work Act 1974.

Often called CHIP2, they revoke and replace the Chemical (Hazard Information and Packaging) Regulations 1993 SI 1993/1746

Allow a transitional period until 31st July 1995 from CHIP1 to CHIP2.

These Regulations require chemicals to be classified in a particular way and then suitably packaged and labelled and accompanied by a safety data sheet.

Comprehensive guidance is available from HSE Books.

Cinematograph (Safety) Regulations 1955
SI 1955/1129

Commencement: 1st January 1956

Apply to England, Wales, and Scotland.

Maintained in force under the later Cinema Act 1985.

Amended by various Statutory Instruments (see Cinema Act).

These Regulations are concerned with film projectors, projection rooms, and rewinding rooms. They deal with electrical safety and fire safety. The electrical installation is dealt with in some detail, from wiring to fuses, switches and earths. Emergency lighting is specified, as is electrical equipment, heating equipment and television equipment.

| **Authorities** | (1) | Local Authorities |
| | (2) | Health and Safety Executive |

Cinematograph Films, Use of Apparatus, Safety of Provisions Order 1924.
SR & O 1924/403

Commencement: 1st May 1924

Applies to England and Wales.

Made under the Celluloid and Cinematograph Film Act 1922. Deals with fire precautions and safe practice with regard to cinematograph apparatus.

| **Authorities** | (1) | Health and Safety Executive |

Clean Air (Emission of Dark Smoke) (Exemption) Regulations 1989
SI 1989/1263

Commencement: 1st October 1989

Apply to England, Wales, and Scotland.

Made under Clean Air Act 1968.

These Regulations exempt certain activities from the provisions of the Clean Air Act 1968.

Clean Air (Emission of Grit and Dust from Furnaces) Regulations 1971
SI 1971/162

Commencement: 1st November 1971

Apply to England, Wales, and Scotland.

Made under the Clean Air Act 1968.

These Regulations prescribe limits on the rates of emission of grit and dust from the chimney of any furnace in which solid, liquid or gaseous matter is burnt. They do not apply to a furnace designed for domestic use and with a heating capacity of less than 55,000 BTU/hr.

Clean Air (Height of Chimneys) (Exemption) Regulations 1969
SI 1969/411

Commencement: 1st April 1969

Apply to England, Wales, and Scotland.

Made under Clean Air Act 1968.

These Regulations exempt some temporary arrangements with regard to heat and power plants from the necessity of having chimneys of a certain height.

Clean Air (Units of Measurement) Regulations 1992
SI 1992/36

Commencement: 5 February 1992

Apply to England, Wales, and Scotland.

Amend Clean Air Acts 1956 and 1968 by metricating the units of mass and power.

Construction (Design and Management) Regulations 1994
SI 1994/3140

Commencement: 31st March 1995 but with a 9 month lead in period

Apply to England, Wales, and Scotland.

Implement the EC Temporary and Mobile Construction Worksites Directive (92/57/EEC)

The Regulations place duties on clients, planning supervisors, principal contractors, designers and contractors to plan, coordinate and manage health and safety at construction sites.

Apply to all notifiable construction sites, ie those which last 30 days or involve more than 500 person days of work.

Authorities   (1)   Health and Safety Executive

Guidance

L54 Management Construction for Health and Safety, Approved Code of Practice, HSE. 1994.

Designing for Health and Safety in Construction, HSE. 1994.

A Guide to Managing Health and Safety in Construction, HSE, 1994.

Guidance for Builders and Constructors - Small Construction Sites, HSE. 1994.

All these are available from HSE Books.

Construction (Head Protection) Regulations 1989
SI 1989/2209

Commencement: 30th March 1990

Apply to England, Wales, and Scotland.

Made under the Health and Safety at Work etc Act 1974.

These Regulations define the type of headgear that should be worn and the type of site for which head protection is required to be worn. This in practice will cover most construction activities.

Authorities   (1)   Health and Safety Executive

Construction (Lifting Operations) Regulations 1961
SI 1961/1581

Commencement: 1st March 1962

Apply to England, Wales, and Scotland.

Made under the Factories Act 1961.

Deal with the construction, maintenance and inspection of lifting machinery and all aspects of their use. All such equipment shall be marked with safe working load.

Reports, certificates etc must be kept and be made available for inspection by HM Inspectors of Factories.

Construction Products Regulations 1991
SI 1991/1620

Commencement: 27th December 1991

Apply to England, Wales, Scotland and Northern Ireland.

Made under the European Communities Act 1972.

A construction product, meaning an item which is incorporated in a permanent manner in works, must satisfy the essential requirements with regard to:-

(1)   Mechanical resistance and stability

(2)   Safety in case of fire

(3)   Hygiene, health and the environment

(4)   Safety in use

(5)   Protection against noise

(6)   Energy economy and heat retention

If the product obtains an EC certificate of conformity this is taken to mean that it has these essential requirements. Otherwise the supplier would have to show to enforcement officers that the product either did satisfy the essential requirements or that the Regulations did not apply.

The mechanisms for awarding the CE mark are not in place at present but when they are, a product bearing it can cross European national frontiers without hindrance. Amended by SI 1994/3051 (in force 1/1/95) which gives effect to European Directive 93/68.

Authorities   (1)   Trading Standards departments of Local Authorities in Great Britain

(2)   Environmental Health Authorities in Northern Ireland

(3)   Department of the Environment

Consumer Protection (Cancellation of Contracts Concluded Away from Business Premises) Regulations 1988
SI 1988/958

Commencement: May 1988

Apply to England, Wales, Scotland and Northern Ireland.

Made under the Consumer Protection Act 1987.

Implement a European Community Directive to protect consumers from contracts made on the doorstep.

Control of Asbestos at Work Regulations 1987
SI 1987/2115

Commencement: 1st March 1988

Apply to England, Wales, and Scotland.

Made under the Health and Safety at Work etc Act 1974.

These regulations revoke the 1969 Asbestos Regulations. They provide protection for anyone working with, or affected by, work involving asbestos. They cover all workplaces. They deal with assessment of exposure, and its prevention, reduction and control; adequate information, instruction and training for employees; monitoring and health surveillance.

Amended by the Control of Asbestos at Work (Amendment) Regulations 1992 SI 1992/3068. In effect 1/1/93. Introduce among other controls, a 'plan of work' for asbestos removal work. Employee health records must be kept for 40 years.

An approved Code of Practice "Control of Asbestos at Work" Health and Safety Executive, HMSO. 1983, gives practical guidance to the requirements of the Regulations.

Control of Asbestos in the Air Regulations 1990
SI 1990/556

Commencement: 5th April 1990

Apply to England, Wales, and Scotland.

Made under the Health and Safety at Work etc Act 1974.

The main provisions of these regulations are to prescribe a limit value for the discharge of asbestos from outlets into the air ($0.1mg/m^3$ air) and to provide for regular measurement of asbestos emissions. They also provide for the control of environmental pollution by asbestos emitted into the air from the working of products or the demolition of buildings.

Control of Industrial Major Accident Hazards Regulations 1984
SI 1984/1902

Commencement: 8th January 1985 (Regulations 6-10) 1st April 1985 (Remainder)

Apply to England, Wales, Scotland and Northern Ireland.

Made under the European Communities Act 1972 and the Health and Safety at Work Act 1974.

The aim of these Regulations is to identify and register dangerous industrial activities and to set up emergency plans to deal with them. A major accident is a major emission, fire or explosion in industry, which may present a serious danger to persons, and involving a dangerous substance.

These Regulations are amended by SI 1994/118 with a similar name, which came into force 28th February 1994, which changed compliance dates and transitional provisions.

Control of Lead at Work Regulations 1980
SI 1980/1248

Commencement: 18th August 1981

Apply to England, Wales, and Scotland.

Made under the Health and Safety at Work etc Act 1974.

These Regulations apply to any work with lead to which the Health and Safety at Work etc Act 1974 applies.

Authorities   (1)   Health and Safety Executive

Cited Standards etc

Approved Code of Practice "Control of Lead at Work", Health and Safety Executive,HMSO, 1980.

Control of Noise (Code of Practice for Construction Sites) Order 1975
SI 1975/2115

Commencement: 1st January 1976

Applies to England, Wales, and Scotland.

Made under the Control of Pollution Act 1974.

Provide for the issue and enforcement of a Code of Practice on this topic.

Cited Standards etc

Code of Practice BS 5228:1975.

Control of Noise (Code of Practice on Noise from Audible Intruder Alarms) Order 1981
SI 1981/1829

Commencement: 1st February 1982

Applies to England, Wales, and Scotland.

Made under the Control of Pollution Act 1974.

Provides for the issue and enforcement of a Code of Practice on this topic.

Cited Standards etc

Code of Practice on noise from audible intruder alarms, HMSO, 1982.

Control of Noise (Measurement and Registers) Order 1976
SI 1976/37

Commencement: 13th February 1976

Applies to England, Wales, and Scotland.

Made under the Control of Pollution Act 1974.

Authorities   (1)   Local Authority

Control of Substances Hazardous to Health Regulations 1994
SI 1994/3246

Commencement: 16th January 1995

Apply to England, Wales, and Scotland.

Made under the Health and Safety at Work Act 1974.

These are consolidating Regulations which repeal and replace all previous COSHH Regulations and amendments. The aim of these Regulations is to protect workers' health from hazardous substances used at work. The employer has to assess the risks from such substances, and for certain substances he has to monitor the employee's exposure to them. The 1995 Occupational Exposure Limits EH 40/95 are based on these Regulations.

New and Revised Approved Codes of Practice and other supporting documents are expected in 1995.

Authorities   (1)   Health and Safety Executive

Control of Substances Hazardous to Health Regulations (Northern Ireland) 1995
SR 1995/51

Commencement: 30th March 1995

Apply to Northern Ireland.

Made SI 1978/1039 (NI9).

These Regulations are similar to the England, Wales, Scotland COSHH Regulations (SI 1994/3246) but may not be identical to them.

Authorities   (1)   Health and Safety Agency for Northern Ireland

Controlled Waste (Registration of Carriers and Seizure of Vehicles) Regulations 1991
SI 1991/1624

Commencement: 14th October 1991

Apply to England, Wales, and Scotland.

Made under the Environmental Protection Act 1990.

Concerns registration of a carrier of controlled waste under the Environmental Protection Act 1990 and the penalties for non-registration by those required to do so.

Amended by the Trans Frontier Shipment of Waste Regulations 1994 (qv)

Authorities   (1)   Waste Regulation Authority

Guidance Note

"Waste Management - The Duty of Care - A Code of Practice", Department of the Environment, 1990, HMSO.

Disposal of Controlled Waste (Exceptions) Regulations 1991
SI 1991/508

Commencement: England and Wales 1st April 1991, Scotland 1st April 1992

Apply to England, Wales, and Scotland.

Made under the Control of Pollution Act 1974.

These Regulations are concerned with potential overlaps between the Control of Pollution Act 1974 and the Environmental Protection Act 1990.

Education (School Premises) Regulations 1981
SI 1981/909

Commencement: 1st August 1981

Apply to England, Wales, and Scotland.

Made under the Education Act 1944.

Regulations concerned with building services to schools.

Authorities   (1)   Department for Education
                         (2)   Local Authorities

Cited Standards etc

Guidelines for the Environmental Design of Fuel Conservction in Educational Buildings, Department of Education and Science, Design Note 17, 1981.

EEC Council Regulation "Substances that deplete the ozone layer"
EEC 594/91 amended by EEC 3952/92

Commencement: 30th December 1992 by virtue of the European Communities Act 1972

Apply to England, Wales, Scotland and Northern Ireland.

This Regulation commits each member of the European Union to reduce in stages the production and importation of CFCs and halons (as defined by the Montreal Protocol) to zero. Additionally all fully halogenated chlorofluorocarbons were added and given the same time-table of production as CFCs. Two new chemicals, carbon tetrachloride and 1;1;1 trichloroethane were also given dates for production and importation limitation and cessation.

The Council Regulation 95/107/EC extends controls to hydrochlorofluorocarbons (HCFCs) and hydrobromofluorcarbons (HBFCs) and to methyl bromide.

Authorities   (1)   Department of the Environment

                         (2)   European Commission

Electrical Equipment (Safety) Regulations 1994
SI 1994/3260

Commencement: 9th January 1995

Apply to England, Wales, Scotland and Northern Ireland.

Made under European Communities Act 1974 and Consumer Protection Act 1987.

All new items on the market from 1st January 1997 must conform to these Regulations. Up to then transitional arrangements apply where compliance with the Low Voltage Electrical Equipment (Safety) Regulations 1989 *(Page 75)* is sufficient.

Electrically, Hydraulically and Oil-Electrically Operated Lifts (Components) (EEC Requirements) Regulations 1991
SI 1991/2748

Commencement: 1st January 1992

Apply to England, Wales, Scotland and Northern Ireland.

These Regulations revoke the Electrically Operated Lifts (EEC Requirements) Regulations 1986. They provide for testing and certification of all the types of lifts mentioned in the regulation title.

Authorities   (1)   Secretary of State for Trade and Industry

Electricity at Work Regulations 1989
SI 1989/635

Commencement: 1st April 1990

Apply to England, Wales, and Scotland.

Made under the Health and Safety at Work etc Act 1974.

These Regulations impose health and safety requirements with respect to electricity at work. They impose duties on employers etc. They impose requirements as to systems, work activities and protective equipment. Compliance with the current IEE wiring regulations (BS 7671:1992) is likely to achieve compliance with these regulations as far as design and construction is concerned.

Guidance Note

Memorandum of Guidance on the Electricity at Work Regulations 1989 (HS(R)25), HMSO.

Electromagnetic Compatibility Regulations 1992
SI 1992/2372

Commencement: 28th October 1992

Apply to England, Wales, Scotland and Northern Ireland.

Made under the European Communities Act 1972.

These Regulations implement Council Directive 89/336/EEC as amended by 92/31/EEC.

These Regulations cover all electrical and electronic appliances and associated equipment which are liable to cause electromagnetic disturbance or are liable to be affected by such disturbances.

This apparatus must have the essential protection requirements of not interfering with radio or telecommunications equipment, and of being immune enough to electromagnetic disturbance so as to operate as intended.

Up to 31st December 1995 conformity with UK existing legislation is sufficient, eg *(Pages 94 - 95)*, but from 1st January 1997 compliance with these Regulations is necessary.

These have been significantly amended by the Electromagnetic Compatibility (Amendment) Regulations 1994 SI 1994/3080 (in force 5/12/94) which implement European Directive 93/68 as amended, regarding use of the CE mark.

Enforcement

Great Britain   (1)   Trading Standards

                  (2)   Radiocommunications Agency

                  (3)   Civil Aviation Authority

                  (4)   Director General of Electricity Supply

Northern Ireland (1)   Department of Economic Development

                  (2)   Director General of Electricity Supply for Northern
                          Ireland

Energy Information (Refrigeration and Freezers) Regulations 1994
SI 1994/3076

Commencement: 1st January 1995

Apply to England, Wales, Scotland and Northern Ireland.

Made under the European Communities Act 1972.

These Regulations impose a duty on the supplier of refrigerators and freezers to
supply the purchaser with their energy consumption information. The supplier is
also responsible for the accuracy of the information. Implement European
Directives 92/75, 95/2.

Authorities   (1)   Trading Standards Officer

Environmental Assessment (Scotland) Regulations 1988
SI 1988/1221 (S122)

Commencement: 15th July 1988

Apply to Scotland.

Made under the European Communities Act 1972.

Cover planning, electricity applications, specific development in new towns,
drainage works, and amend the Roads (Scotland) Act 1984. Schedule 2 sets out the
descriptions of development affected, mostly of an industrial and commercial type.

These Regulations were amended by SI 1994/2012 (S91) which implements European Council Directive 85/337/EEC in Scotland. These add new clauses to Schedule 2 mentioned above to include, a wind generator, a motorway service area and coast protection works.

Environmental Protection (Applications, Appeals and Registers) Regulations 1991
SI 1991/507

Commencement: 1st April 1991

Apply to England, Wales, and Scotland.

Made under the Environmental Protection Act 1990.

Regulate the procedures to be followed for authorisation under the Act.

Environmental Protection (Authorisation of Processes) (Determination Periods) Order 1991
SI 1991/513

Commencement: 1st April 1991

Applies to England and Wales.

Made under the Environmental Protection Act 1990.

This Regulation as amended by SI 1994/2847 (in force 1/12/94) varies the period available to enforcing authorities to consider applications for authorisation.

Environmental Protection (Controls of Injurious Substances) Regulations 1992
SI 1992/31

Commencement: 28th February 1992

Apply to England and Wales.

Made under the Environmental Protection Act 1990.

These Regulations give effect to part of a Council Directive (89/677/EEC). They amend the Control of Pollution (Supply and Use of Injurious Substances)

Regulations 1986 and prohibit the supply and use of preparations or waste containing polychlorinated biphenyl (PCB) or polychlorinated terphenyl (PCT).

The Regulations prohibit the sale or use of certain lead paints (unless used to restore certain historic artifacts), and certain mercury arsenic and organo-tin compounds.

Environmental Protection (Controls of Injurious Substances) (No. 2) Regulations 1993
SI 1993/1643

Commencement: 31st July 1993

Apply to England, Wales, Scotland and Northern Ireland.

Made under the European Communities Act 1972.

Introduce a 2-year transition period for these controls, one of which bans and limits the use of cadmium.

Environmental Protection (Determination of Enforcing Authority etc.) (Scotland) Regulations 1992
SI 1992/530

Commencement: 1st April 1992

Apply to Scotland.

Made under the Environmental Protection Act 1990.

Regulations which provide demarcation between enforcing authorities in Scotland depending on whether a prescribed substance is released in water or air.

Authorities	(1)	Chief Inspector (Air)
	(2)	River Purification Authority (Water)

Environmental Protection (Duty of Care) Regulations 1991
SI 1991/2839

Commencement: 1st April 1992

Apply to England and Wales.

Made under the Environmental Protection Act 1990.

Concern the transfer of written description of waste as the waste goes from one person to another, and the duty to keep copies of the transfer note for 2 years.

Authorities   (1)   Waste Regulation Authority

Environmental Protection (Non-Refillable Refrigerant Containers) Regulations 1994
SI 1994/199

Commencement: 2nd March 1994

Apply to England and Wales.

Made under the Environmental Protection Act 1990.

Impose restrictions on importation, supply and storage of non-refillable containers containing certain chlorofluorcarbons (CFCs) and hydrochlorofluorocarbons (HCFCs) for use as refrigerants in air conditioning and refrigeration machinery.

Environmental Protection (Proscribed Processes and Substances) Regulations 1991
SI 1991/472

Commencement: 1st April 1991

Apply to England and Wales.

Made under the Environmental Protection Act 1990.

These Regulations list the processes and substances which are subject to Integrated Pollution Control (IPC) and local authority air pollution control under the Act. A timetable for each industry to apply for an authorisation is also included.

Amended by SI 1992/614, SI 1993/1749, SI 1993/2405 and SI 1994/1271 (in force 1/6/94)

Authorities   (Depend on class of process)

                         1)   Her Majesty's Inspectorate of Pollution

                         2)   Local Authorities

Examination of Steam Boilers Regulations 1964
SI 1964/781

Commencement: 27th June 1964

Apply to England, Wales, and Scotland.

Made under the Factories Act 1961.

The Regulations govern the manner of examination and the intervals between examinations of steam boilers. In 1981 there was an amendment which metricated the steam flow rates given in Section 4 of these regulations.

Fire Precautions (Application for a Certificate) Regulations 1989
SI 1989/77

Commencement: 1st April 1989

Apply to England, Wales, and Scotland.

Made under the Fire Precautions Act 1971.

These Regulations revoke SI 1976/2008 of the same name and prescribe a new form of application for a fire certificate under the Act. Information such as the number of persons at work and fire precautions present needs to be supplied. Apply to all buildings not covered by other Acts.

Fire Precautions (Factories, Offices, Shops and Railway Premises) Order 1989
SI 1989/76

Commencement: 1st April 1989

Applies to England, Wales, and Scotland.

Made under the Fire Precautions Act 1971.

Revokes a previous regulation of same name SI 1976/2009.

Deals with the fire certificate requirements for factories, offices, shops and railway premises.

Authorities   (1)   Health and Safety Executive

                         (2)   Fire Authority

Fire Precautions (Hotels and Boarding Houses) Order 1972
SI 1972/238

Commencement: 1st June 1972

Applies to England, Wales, and Scotland.

Made under the Fire Precautions Act 1971.

The Order deals with fire certificates for hotels and boarding houses with provision for loans to obtain compliance.

Authorities (1) Fire Authority

       (2) Health and Safety Executive

       (3) Local Authorities

Fire Precautions (Non-certified Factory, Office, Shops and Railway Premises) (Revocation) Regulations 1989
SI 1989/78

Commencement: 1st April 1989

Apply to England, Wales, and Scotland.

Made under the Fire Precautions Act 1971.

These regulations revoke SI 1976/2010 of similar title - which required fire precautions on premises not requiring a certificate under above Act.

Fire Precautions (Places of Work) Regulations

Commencement: Not in force yet

Apply to England, Wales, and Scotland.

Made under the Fire Precautions Act 1971.

The responsibility for fire precautions lies with the employer who must make a fire-risk assessment. Escape routes must be adequate, signposted and preserved. These Regulations concern fighting fires, detecting fires, maintenance testing information and training. They also have a section on assisting people with disabilities.

Fire Precautions (Sub-surface Railway Stations) Regulations 1989
SI 1989/1401

Commencement: partly 18th September 1988; partly 1st January 1990; partly 1st January 1991; fully 1st January 1996

Apply to England, Wales and Scotland.

Made under the Fire Precautions Act 1971.

These Regulations provide for fire precautions to be taken in underground and low-level stations of a specific description, used by members of the public. Cover escape, firefighting equipment, fire detection, zoning, training of staff, construction, no-smoking, maintenance, record keeping.

Amended by SI 1994/2184 (1/1/96)

Fire Precautions Act 1971 (Modification) (Revocation) Regulations 1989
SI 1989/78

Commencement: 1st April 1989

Apply to England, Wales, and Scotland.

Made under the Health and Safety at Work etc Act 1974.

These Regulations modify the Fire Precautions Act 1971 by removing a previous modification SI 1976/2007.

Food Hygiene (Amendment) Regulations 1990
SI 1990/1431

Commencement: 1st April 1991

Apply to England, Wales, and Scotland.

Made under the Food Safety Act 1990.

These Regulations amended the Food Hygiene (General) Regulations 1970 SI 1970/1172. They concern the hygienic preparation, handling and sale of food intended for human consumption. They cover facilities to be provided in food preparation, behaviour of food handlers and temperature control for storage of relevant foods. These foods have to be stored below 8°C (below 5°C from 1

April 1993 for certain foods) or above 63°C. Temperatures refer to the food and not to its environment. Crown premises are included.

The Food Hygiene (Markets, Stalls and Delivery Vehicles) Regulations 1966 have been amended to include delivery vehicles of all sizes.

Authorities   (1)   Trading Standards Officers

(2)   Environmental Health Officers

(3)   Department of the Environment (for policy decisions)

Food Hygiene (Amendment) Regulations 1991
SI 1991/1343

Commencement: 5th July 1991

Apply to England, Wales, and Scotland.

Made under the Food Safety Act 1990.

These Regulations amend the Food Hygiene (Market, Stalls and Delivery Vehicles) Regulations 1966 and the Food Hygiene (General) Regulations 1970. They bring pies and pastries containing cheese and cakes containing cream/cream substitutes under the temperature controls of the 1990 amendment of a similar title.

Food Premises (Registration) Regulations 1991
SI 1991/2825

Commencement: in stages from February to July 1992

Apply to England, Wales, and Scotland.

Made under the Food Safety Act 1990.

Provide for the registration of food premises by food authorities. Premises must be registered if they are used for carrying on a food business on five or more days (not necessarily consecutive) in a period of five consecutive weeks. Market stalls etc and other mobile premises are subject to the requirement.

Amended by Food Premises (Registration) Amendment Regulations 1993 SI 1993/2022. These exclude child-minder premises from registration.

Authorities   (1)   Environmental Health Officers

Food Safety (General Food Hygiene) Regulations 1995

Commencement: Not in force until at least September 1995

Apply to England, Wales, and Scotland.

Made under the Food Safety Act 1990.

A Draft for public comment has been issued by the Department of Health.

The following legal changes are planned:-

    1)   Suitable training for staff in food hygiene

    2)   Hazard-analysis required for food production areas

    3)   Easing of temperature rules allowing more foods to be held at 8°C

Guidance

Assured Safe Catering, Department of Health, HMSO, 1994.

Fuel and Electricity (Heating) (Control) (Amendment) Order 1980
SI 1980/1013

Commencement: 1st October 1980

Applies to England, Wales, Scotland and Northern Ireland.

Made under the Energy Act 1976.

The Order lowers to 19°C the temperature above which premises may not be heated.

Gas (Meters) Regulations 1983
SI 1983/684

Commencement: 1st January 1973

Apply to England, Wales, and Scotland.

Made under the Gas Act 1972.

Prescribe standards for meters and examination of meters for conformity to these standards.

Authorities   (1)   British Gas.

Gas Appliances (Safety) Regulations 1992
SI 1992/711

Commencement: 6th April 1992

Apply to England, Wales, Scotland and Northern Ireland.

Made under the Consumer Protection Act 1987 and the European Communities Act 1972.

Bring into UK law the EEC Directive 90/396/EEC. They apply to all gas and LPG appliances used for cooking, heating, lighting, refrigeration, hot water and washing, where the water temperature does not exceed 105°C. They also apply to their fittings, controls and sub-assemblies.

Up to July 1995 these products must either conform to the existing laws or the essential requirements of these Regulations but after 1st January 1996 all products must comply with the essential requirements only and carry the CE mark.

Authorities	(1)	Local Trading Standards Offices for Domestic Appliances
	(2)	Health and Safety Inspectors for Appliances for Use in Work-Places

Gas Catalytic Heaters (Safety) Regulations 1984
SI 1984/1802

Commencement: 21st November 1984

Apply to England, Wales, Scotland and Northern Ireland.

Made under the Consumer Protection Act 1987.

Prohibit heaters which employ unbonded asbestos catalytic units or contain any asbestos for insulation or otherwise.

Authorities	(1)	Health and Safety Executive
	(2)	Local Authority

Gas Cooking Appliances (Safety) Regulations 1989
SI 1989/149

Commencement: partly 1st March 1989, fully 1st September 1989

Apply to England, Wales, Scotland and Northern Ireland.

Made under the Consumer Protection Act 1987.

These Regulations prohibit the supply of gas cooking appliances which do not comply with the conditions set out in the Regulations, or with European Standard EN30 or British Standard BS 5386 Part 3 1980 or Part 4 1983.

Gas Safety (Installation and Use) Regulations 1994
SI 1994/1886

Commencement: In stages from 31st October 1994 to 1st January 1997

Apply to England, Wales, and Scotland.

Made under the Gas Act.

Deal with safety, installation and use of gas fittings. Cover all aspects of gas transmission, distribution, supply or use, including gas from a gas storage vessel in some cases.

Certain premises are exempt being covered by their own Regulations, eg mines, quarries, factories, agricultural premises or temporary installations.

Require carbon monoxide detection to be fitted to appliances which can cut off gas supply if levels get too high. Landlords must maintain gas appliances annually.

Previous Regulations of the similar name of 1983 and 1990 and their amendments, are revoked.

Authorities   (1)   Health and Safety Executive

                             (2)   Local Authorities

                             (3)   British Gas

Cited Standards etc

Safety in the Installation and Use of Gas Systems and Appliances (L56), Approved Code of Practice and Guidance, HSE Books, HMSO, 1994.

Gas Safety (Installation and Use) Regulations (Northern Ireland) 1995
SR 1995/3

Commencement: 1995

Apply to Northern Ireland.

These Regulations are more or less the same as the equivalent ones for England, Wales and Scotland. Whilst generally there is no public gas supply in Northern Ireland and people use gas from containers, it is expected that some natural gas will be brought on shore from local gas fields, for industrial use.

Gas Safety Regulations 1972
SI 1972/1172

Commencement: 1st December 1972

Apply to England, Wales, and Scotland.

Made under the Gas Act 1948 and maintained by the Gas Act 1972.

These Regulations allow the Secretary of State for Trade and Industry to make safety regulations with regard to gas appliances and gas use for the UK. These Regulations were amended in 1976 SI 1976/1982 and in 1983 SI 1983/1575 and in 1994 by SI 1994/1886.

General Product Safety Regulations 1994
SI 1994/2328

Commencement: 3rd October 1994

Apply to England, Wales and Scotland.

Made under the European Communities Act 1972.

Apply to both new and secondhand products. Antiques, and products supplied that are in need of repair are not covered by the Regulations, provided the purchaser is clearly informed of this fact. They provide a common framework for assessing the safety of products.

Health and Safety (Display Screen Equipment) Regulations 1992
SI 1992/2792

Commencement: 1st January 1993

Apply to England, Wales, and Scotland.

Made under the Health and Safety at Work etc Act 1974.

Apply to display screens which the employee habitually uses for a significant part of normal work. The employer has to assess the risks of using display equipment workstations and supply a workstation which satisfies minimum requirements for ease of use. The work should be arranged so that there are breaks or changes of activity.

Guidance Note

Display Screen Equipment Work: A Guide to the Regulations, HMSO, 1992.

Health and Safety (Emissions into the Atmosphere) Regulations 1983
SI 1983/943 and Amendment 1989 SI 1989/319

Commencement: 5th August 1983

Apply to England, Wales, and Scotland.

Made under the Health and Safety at Work etc Act 1974.

These Regulations prescribe certain classes of premises from which emissions into the atmosphere may be controlled. They also prescribe certain substances which are to be treated as noxious or offensive. A duty is imposed of preventing or neutralising these emissions.

Highly Flammable Liquid and Liquefied Petroleum Gases Regulations 1972

SI 1972/917

Commencement: 21st June 1973 and 21st June 1974 (one section)

Apply to England, Wales, and Scotland.

Made under the Factories Act 1961.

Concern storage, use, labelling and safe practices required in handling highly flammable liquid and liquefied petroleum gases in workplaces. A highly flammable liquid is one with a flashpoint below 35°C.

Authorities   (1)   Factories Inspectorate

Hoists Exemption Order 1962
SI 1962/715

Commencement: 16th April 1962

Applies to England, Wales and Scotland.

Made under the Factories Act 1961.

Provide for a number of exceptions and exemptions to the requirements of the Factories Act 1961.

Home Energy Efficiency Grants Regulations 1992
SI 1992/483

Commencement: 1st April 1992

Apply to England, Wales and Scotland

Made under the Social Security Act 1990.

Provide for grants for the improvement of energy efficiency for dwellings occupied by persons on low income for certain buildings in multiple occupation.

Amended by SI 1993/2799 (9/12/93) and by SI 1994/637 (1/4/94)

Housing (Means of Escape from Fire in Houses in Multiple Occupation) Order 1981
SI 1981/1576

Commencement: 3rd December 1981

Applies to England and Wales.

Made under the Housing Act 1980.

Provide that local authorities require houses in multiple occupancy to be provided with means of escape from fire. It covers buildings of three storeys or more with a total floor area greater than 500m^2.

Authorities   (1)   Local Authorities

                       (2)   Fire Authorities

Ionising Radiations Regulations 1985
SI 1985/1333

Commencement: partly 1st October 1985, fully 1st January 1986

Apply to England, Wales, and Scotland.

Made under the Health and Safety at Work etc Act 1974.

The Regulations concern work with radioactive substances and ionising radiations regarding exposure to radon.

Authorities   (1)   Health and Safety Executive (HSE)

Codes of Practice

Exposure to Radon. The Ionising Radiation Regulations 1985. Part 3. Approved Code of Practice, COP23, HSE, HMSO, 1988.

The Protection of Persons Against Ionising Radiations Arising From Any Work Activity, COP16, HSE, HMSO, 1985.

Ionising Radiations (Outside Workers) Regulations 1993
SI 1993/2379

Commencement: 1st January 1994

Apply to England, Wales and Scotland.

Made under the European Communities Act 1972 and the Health and Safety at Work Act 1974.

Deal with the duties of outside undertakings, radiation pass books, duties of operation and outside workers, enforcement and exemptions.

Amended by a correction slip.

Lifting Plant and Equipment (Record of Test and Examinations etc) Regulations 1992
SI 1992/195

Commencement: 30th April 1992

Apply to England, Wales and Scotland.

Made under Health and Safety at Work Act 1974.

Radically simplify the record keeping requirement associated with test and examination results. The testing obligations are unchanged. Records no longer have to be kept on prescribed forms, but can be kept either in writing or electronic format.

Low Voltage Electrical Equipment (Safety) Regulations 1989
SI 1989/728

Commencement: 1st June 1989

Apply to England, Wales, Scotland and Northern Ireland.

Made under the Consumer Protection Act 1987.

Implements EEC Directive 73/23.

Apply to any electrical equipment for use on 50-1000 Volts AC with some exclusions.

These Regulations harmonise the laws of EEC member states with respect to electrical equipment which runs on low voltage. The equipment has to satisfy safety provisions approved in accordance with the Approval of Safety Standard Regulations 1987 SI 1987/1911. The supply of equipment which does not satisfy these conditions is prohibited.

Management of Health and Safety at Work Regulations 1992
SI 1992/2051

Commencement: 1st January 1993

Apply in England, Wales and Scotland.

Made under the Health and Safety at Work etc Act 1974.

These Regulations require employers to assess risks to health and safety and record findings. Having done so they must implement measures to control risks, appoint competent people, set up emergency procedures and provide information and training for employees and anyone else who needs to know.

Employees have to use equipment in accordance with training and have the duty to report dangerous situations to their employers.

Amended by Management of Health and Safety at Work (Amendment) Regulations 1994 SI 1994/2865 (in force 1/12/94) which implement the Pregnant Workers Directive (92/85/EEC). The Health and Safety Executive is expected to provide guidance on this amendment.

Guidance Note

Management of Health and Safety at Work: Approved Code of Practice (ACOP), HMSO, 1992.

COP26. Rider-operated lift trucks - Operator training: Approved Code of Practice and Supplementary Guidance. HSE 1994.

Manual Handling Operations Regulations 1992
SI 1992/2793

Commencement: 1st January 1993

Apply to England, Wales, and Scotland.

Made under the Health and Safety at Work etc Act 1974.

These Regulations apply to any manual handling operations which may cause injury at work. These operations will be identified by the risk assessment carried out under the Management of the Health and Safety at Work Regulations 1992. *(Page 75)*

Guidance Note

Work Equipment. Guidance on Regulations, HMSO, 1992.

Marketing of Gas Oil (Sulphur Content) Regulations 1994
SI 1994/2249

Commencement: 1st October 1994

Apply to England, Wales and Scotland.

Made under the European Communities Act 1972.

These Regulations prohibit the marketing of gas oil with a sulphur content exceeding 0.2% by weight. The method of measurement is defined. They revoke previous Regulations on sulphur content SI 1990/1096 and SR (NI 1991/235)

Authorities   (1)   Local Authorities

Measuring Instruments (EEC Requirements) (Electrical Energy Meters) Regulations 1986
S1 1986/886

Commencement: 22nd July 1980

Apply to England, Wales, Scotland and Northern Ireland.

Made under the European Communities Act 1972.

Make the EEC-approved meters eligible for UK use if they have an EEC initial verification mark.

Measuring Instruments (EEC Requirements) (Gas Volume Meters) Regulations 1983
SI 1983/1246

Commencement: 6th September 1983

Apply to England, Wales, Scotland and Northern Ireland.

Made under the European Communities Act 1972.

Make the EEC-approved gas volume meters eligible for UK use. Implementation of an EEC Council Directive 718/318.

Noise at Work Regulations 1989
SI 1989/1790

Commencement: 1st January 1990

Apply to England, Wales, and Scotland.

Made under the Health and Safety at Work etc Act 1974.

These Regulations require employers to:-

(a) Assess the employee's exposure to noise

(b) Keep a record of such assessment to be kept

(c) Reduce noise risks

(d) Provide ear protection

(e) Mark zones which require ear protection

(f) Maintain equipment

(g) Provide information and training

Based on EC Directive 86/188/EEC.

Guidance Note

Noise in Construction (IND(G) 127(L)). Available free from HSE Books.

Noise Insulation (Amendment) Regulations 1988
SI 1988/2000

Commencement: 20th November 1988

Made under the Land Compensation Act 1973.

Apply to England, Wales, and Scotland.

These amendments update references to other legislation and codes in the Noise Insulation Regulations 1975.

Noise Insulation Regulations 1975
SI 1975/1763

Commencement: 7th November 1975

Apply to England and Wales.

Made under the Land Compensation Act 1973.

These Regulations concern the grants to provide noise insulation which are available to householders and others who suffer from traffic noise.

Authorities   (1)   Local Authority

                       (2)   Secretary of State for the Environment

Cited Standards etc

Technical Memorandum " Calculation of Road Traffic Noise", Department of the Environment, HMSO, 1975.

Notification of Cooling Towers and Evaporative Condensers Regulations 1992
SI 1992/2225

Commencement: 2nd November 1992

Apply to England, Wales, and Scotland.

Made under the Health and Safety at Work etc Act 1974.

These Regulations require all premises containing a cooling tower or evaporative condenser to be notified to the local authority in whose area the building is situated. A form is available from the Environmental Health Departments of local authorities. Notification must also be given of changes to the information supplied.

Authorities   (1)   Local Authority

Notification of New Substances Regulations 1993
SI 1993/3050

Commencement: 31st January 1994

Apply to England, Wales and Scotland.

Made under the European Communities Act 1972.

Replace the 1992 Regulations of the same name and subsequent amendments. They implement certain requirements of EC Amendment (92/32/EEC) to the Dangerous Substances Directive.

Suppliers are requested to inform a competent authority (HSE and DOE in the UK) of their intention to place a new substance on the market and to provide information about it. The competent authority is required to carry out a risk assessment and make recommendations as necessary for its control.

There is European Inventory of Existing Commercial Chemical Substances available from HMSO.

Nursing Homes and Mental Nursing Homes Regulations 1984
SI 1984/1578 and SI 1986/456

Commencement: 1st January 1985

Apply to England, Wales, and Scotland.

Made under the Registered Homes Act 1984.

The Regulations concern facilities and services in nursing homes, for example emergency electrical supply, heating, lighting, fire precautions and waste disposal.

Authorities   (1)   Fire Authorities

                         (2)   Health Authority

Offices, Shops and Railway Premises (Hoist and Lifts) Regulations 1968
SI 1968/849

Commencement: 28th May 1968

Apply to England, Wales and Scotland.

Made under the Offices, Shops and Railway Premises Act 1963.

Require hoists and lifts to be properly constructed of sound material and adequate strength. They must be properly maintained.

Off-shore Installations (Emergency Pipeline Valve) Regulations 1984
SI 1989/1029

Commencement: 12th July 1989

Apply to England, Wales, Scotland and Northern Ireland.

Made under the Mineral Workings (Off-shore Installations) Act 1971 and the Petroleum and Submarine Pipe-lines Act 1975.

These Regulations provide for the protection of off-shore installations which are connected to a pipeline conveying flammable or toxic substances. These require an emergency shut-down valve and provide for its periodic inspection and testing.

Off-shore Installations (Safety Case) Regulations 1992
SI 1992/2885

Commencement: 31st May 1993 (new installations) 20th November 1995 (existing installations)

Apply to England, Wales and Scotland.

Made under the Health and Safety at Work Act 1974.

Owners and operators of off-shore installation must prepare safety cases for each installation and submit them to the Health and Safety Executive.

Oil Fuel (Sulphur Content of Gas Oil) Regulations 1976
SI 1976/1988

Commencement: 29th December 1976

Made under the Control of Pollution Act 1974.

Apply to England, Wales, and Scotland.

No person may use or cause to be used, in any furnace or engine (other than in a power station, ship or diesel engine motor vehicle) any gas oil containing more sulphur than 0.8% weight from 29th December 1976 and more than 0.5% from 1 October 1980 onwards.

There is another Regulation for motor fuel which sets its sulphur content at a lower level than the above.

Oil Heaters (Safety) Regulations 1977
SI 1977/167
(NB. Due for revision under the same name)

Commencement: 1st April 1977

Apply to England, Wales, Scotland and Northern Ireland.

Made under the Consumer Protection Act 1961.

These Regulations concern the safety aspects of the operation of both pressure and gravity-fed oil heaters. They concern warnings and instructions, tests, safe temperatures of surfaces, emissions, fuel temperatures and fuel regulation.

Cited Standards etc

British Standard BS 3300: 1974. Replaced by BS 3300: 1985 but remains current until this Regulation is revoked and replaced by Regulations under the Consumer Safety Act 1978.

Ozone Monitoring and Information Regulations 1994
SI 1994/440

Commencement: 21st March 1994

Apply to England, Wales, and Scotland.

Made under the European Communities Act 1972.

Allow the Secretary of State to establish measuring stations and to use a reference method to measure ozone concentrations. The public must be informed if certain threshold levels, specified in the Council Directive 92/72/EEC, are exceeded.

Personal Protection Equipment (EC Directive) Regulations 1992
SI 1992/3139

Commencement: 1st January 1993

Apply to England, Wales, and Scotland.

Made under the European Communities Act 1972.

Implement EEC Directive 89/686. Make provision for powers to serve prohibition notices etc and for certification and monitoring of sales and free movement of goods around Europe. Amended by SI 1993/3074 to exclude motor cycle helmets and visors.

Personal Protective Equipment (EC Directive) (Amendment) Regulations 1994
SI 1994/2326

Commencement: 1st October 1994 for Regulation 2, remainder 1st January 1995

Apply to England, Wales, and Scotland.

Made under the European Communities Act 1972.

Amend Provision and Use of Work Equipment Regulations 1992 SI 1992/2932, Personal Protective Equipment at Work Regulations 1992 SI 1992/2966, Personal Protective Equipment at Work Regulations (Northern Ireland) 1993 SR 1993/20, Personal Protective Equipment (EC Directive) Regulations 1992 SI 1992/3139. Revoke 1993 Amendment SI 1993/3074.

Regulation 2 brings up to date EC Directive references and is revoked on 1st January 1995 when the CE marking and further updates are introduced.

Personal Protective Equipment at Work Regulations 1992
SI 1992/2966

Commencement: 1st January 1993

Apply to England, Wales and Scotland.

The main Regulation SI 1992/2966 was passed under the Health and Safety at Work etc Act 1974 to implement the European Directive 89/656/EEC.

Personal Protective Equipment (PPE) is defined as all equipment designed to be worn or held to protect against a hazard at work. PPE should be relied on as a last resort but PPE should be suitable for both the risk and the user. The employer has a duty to provide and maintain PPE and ensure it is properly used.

These Regulations do not apply to processes covered by other Regulations, which means they do not cover hearing protection or respiratory protective equipment.

Standards for PPE were established by the Personal Protective Equipment (EC Directive) Regulations 1992 SI 1992/3139 as amended by SI 1993/3074 (in conformity with European Directive 89/684/EEC). Whilst these Regulations came into effect on 1st January 1993 the amendment delayed implementation, allowing a transition period up to 30th June 1995. After this date virtually all PPE should carry the CE mark.

Authorities   (1)   Trading Standards Departments of Local Authorities

Cited Standards etc

1)   Personal Protective Equipment at Work, HMSO, 1991

2)   Product Standards DTI Hot Line 0117-9444888

Planning (Hazardous Substances) Regulations 1992
SI 1992/656

Commencement: 1st June 1992

Apply to England and Wales.

Made under the Planning (Hazardous Substances) Act 1990.

Require a hazardous substance consent to be obtained where a controlled quantity of a hazardous substance is present on, over, or under land. The Regulations list the hazardous substances and the controlled quantities, covered by the 1990 Act *(Page 12)* and provide for consent exemptions etc.

Authorities   (1)   Hazardous Substances Authority

                         (2)   Secretary of State

Plugs and Sockets etc (Safety) Regulations 1994
SI 1994/1768

Commencement: 3rd August 1994 except for parts which come into force 1st February 1995 and finally all comes into force by 1st February 1996

Apply to England, Wales and Scotland.

Made under the Consumer Protection Act 1987.

These Regulations will, when fully applied, ensure that plugs and sockets, fuses etc conform with relevant British and European Standards when offered for sale, even as part of equipment.

Authorities   (1)   Local Authorities

Pressure Systems and Transportable Gas Containers Regulations 1989
SI 1989/2169

Commencement: 1st July 1990, mostly. Other parts 1st January 1991 and finally section 8-12, 1st July 1994

Apply to England, Wales, and Scotland.

Made under the Health and Safety at Work etc. Act 1974.

These Regulations impose safety requirements with respect to pressure systems and transportable gas containers which are used or intended for use at work. They also impose safety requirements to prevent certain vessels from becoming pressurised. They impose regulations on designers, manufacturers, importers and suppliers with respect to the design and construction of such systems and containers. Nothing must be done in modifications or during maintenance which gives rise to danger. Safety information should be provided by all those connected with provision and maintenance. A periodic inspection by a competent person is required and records kept.

Guidance Notes

(a)   Regulations concerning the International Carriage of Dangerous Goods by Rail (RID) ISBN 0-11-550814-7, HMSO.

(b)   The International Maritime Dangerous Goods Code. From the International Maritime Organisation, 4 Albert Embankment, SE1 7SR.

(c)   The European Agreement concerning the International Carriage of Dangerous Goods by Road, ISBN 0-11-550 735-3, HMSO.

Provision and Use of Work Equipment Regulations 1992
SI 1992/2932

Commencement: 1st January 1993

Apply to England, Wales, and Scotland.

Made under the Health and Safety at Work etc Act 1974.

These Regulations give a general duty to an employer to supply safe equipment and to give adequate information, instruction and training on its use, taking into consideration the circumstances of its use. Work equipment ranges from screw drivers to any kind of machine.

Guidance Note

Work Equipment. Guidance on Regulations, HMSO, 1992.

Public Information for Radiation Emergencies Regulations 1992
SI 1992/2997

Commencement: 1st January 1993

Apply to England, Wales and Scotland.

Made under the European Communities Act 1972 and the Health and Safety at Work etc Act 1974.

Implement the European Directive 89/618.

Public information must be available and updated covering the fact of radiological emergency and of any intended health protection measures.

Public Service Contracts Regulations 1993
SI 1993/3228

Commencement: 13th January 1994

Apply to England, Wales, and Scotland.

Made under the European Communities Act 1972.

Implement in its entirety Council Directive 92/50/EEC relating to the coordination of procedures for the award of public services contracts.

They define contracting authority in conformity with Public Works Contracts Regulations 1991 and services providers. There is a minimum value of 200,000 ECU for application of these Regulations. They define procedures which must be followed and services providers eligibility.

Services providers must apply to the courts for any breach of duty under these Regulations.

Public Works Contracts Regulations 1991
SI 1991/2680

Commencement: 21st December 1991

Apply to England, Wales, and Scotland.

Made under the European Communities Act 1972.

Aim to coordinate procedures for the award of public works contracts within the EU. Various bodies are called contracting authorities, such as government departments, local authorities, fire and police authorities and the like.

They define procedures for seeking offers for a public works contract. Any default is actionable by the contractor.

Quick Frozen Foodstuffs Regulations 1990
SI 1990/2615

Commencement: 10th January 1991

Apply to England, Wales and Scotland.

Made under the Food Safety Act 1990.

Apply to food frozen by the process known as quick freezing. They cover sale, packaging, labelling and equipment standards. These show the conditions which must be fulfilled to enable the product to be sold for human consumption, and cover temperature requirements. They have been amended by SI 1994/291.

Authorities   (1)   Food Authority

Quick Frozen Foodstuffs (Amendment) Regulations 1994
SI 1994/298

Commencement: 1st September 1994

Apply to England, Wales and Scotland.

Made under the Food Safety Act 1990.

Require manufacturers, storers, transporters, local distributors and retailers of quick-frozen foodstuffs to get appropriate instruments for monitoring and recording the air temperatures in which quick-frozen foodstuffs are stored and transported. Air temperature records have to be kept for at least one year.

Implement two European Directives 92/1/EEC and 92/2/EEC, and amend the Quick Frozen Foodstuffs Regulations 1990 (SI 1990/2615)

Cited Standards etc

A Code of Practice for Enforcement Officers is due to be issued, available from HMSO

Reporting Injuries, Diseases and Dangerous Occurrences Regulations 1985
SI 1985/2023

Commencement: 1st April 1986

Apply to England, Wales, Scotland and Northern Ireland.

Made under the Health and Safety at Work etc Act 1974.

Provide for the notification and reporting of injuries and dangerous occurrences eg death, disease, gas incident. Further provisions cover mines and quarries and the Health and Safety Executive require further information. Particular incidents are detailed, accidents involving, pressure vessels, electrical short circuit, collapse of scaffolding, pipelines.

Proposals are under discussion for a revision in 1995 of these Regulations to produce a single set of comprehensive and cohesive Regulations for the whole industry.

Authorities   (1)   Health and Safety Executive

Residential Care Homes Regulations
SI 1984/1345 and SI 1986/457

Commencement: 1st January 1985

Made under the Registered Homes Act 1984.

Apply to England, Wales, and the Isles of Scilly.

These Regulations make provision in relation to an application for registration. The criteria are people in charge and conduct of the home. Reference must be made to the Fire Authority.

Authorities   (1)   Local Authority

                       (2)   Fire Authority

                       (3)   Environmental Health Authority

Safety Signs Regulations 1980
SI 1980/1471

Commencement: 1st January 1986

Apply to England, Wales, Scotland and Northern Ireland.

Made under the European Communities Act 1972 in response to an EEC Directive. Due to be replaced by the Safety Signs Regulations 1995.

Authorities   (1)   Health and Safety Executive

Cited Standards etc

All safety signs must now conform with BS 5378 part 1.

Safety Signs Regulations 1995

Commencement: Not in force

Apply to England, Wales, Scotland and Northern Ireland.

Due to be published in the near future to implement the EC Directive 'Safety Signs' Directive (92/58/EEC).

They will replace the current Safety Signs Regulations 1980 and harmonise safety signs throughout the EU making it easier for workers who work across national boundaries. Include fire fighting equipment, the marking of pipes and vessels, controlling cranes and the storage of dangerous substances amongst other things.

Sanitary Accommodation Regulations 1938
SI 1938/311

Commencement: 1st July 1938

Apply to England, Wales, and Scotland.

Made under the Factories Act 1937 and still in force although this Act was repealed by the Factories Act 1961.

These Regulations cover toilets for factories. They state that toilets should be "sufficiently ventilated" and that they should not communicate directly with any workroom. These Regulations were amended in 1974 SI 1974/426.

Sanitary Conveniences Regulations 1964
SI 1964/966

Commencement: 1st January 1966

Apply to England, Wales, and Scotland.

Made under the Offices, Shops, Railway Premises Act 1963.

In premises where the above Act applies suitable and sufficient sanitary conveniences should be supplied. Certain small buildings and structures are excluded.

Simple Pressure Vessels (Safety) Regulations 1991
SI 1991/2749

Commencement: 31st December 1991

Apply to England, Wales, and Scotland.

Made under Health and Safety at Work etc Act 1974. Implementing EC Directive 87/404/EEC.

A simple pressure vessel is defined as a welded vessel intended to contain air or nitrogen at a gauge pressure greater than 0.5 bar. The Regulations concern safety requirements which must be satisfied before a vessel can be taken into service.

These Regulations have been amended by the Simple Pressure Vessels (Safety) (Amendment) Regulations 1994 SI 1994/3098 particularly for CE marking and taking in the expansion of the European Community.

Authorities   (1)   Health and Safety Executive

Supply of Machinery (Safety) Regulations 1992
SI 1992/3073

Commencement: 1st January 1993

Apply to England, Wales, and Scotland.

Made under the Health and Safety at Work etc. Act 1974.

These Regulations put into effect in the UK EEC Council Directives. They apply to relevant machinery, of which some of the more dangerous are listed in Schedule 4, and there are exclusions in Schedule 5.

Relevant machinery must be supplied safe and shown to be so and must be capable of being erected and put into service safely. A CE mark when properly affixed is deemed to satisfy the requirements, but there are other methods of satisfying them.

The Department of Trade and Industry have issued a free explanatory booklet 'Product Standards - Machinery'.

Amended by Supply of Machinery (Safety) (Amendment) Regulations 1994 SI 1994/2063 (in force 1/9/94 except Regulation 4 and Schedule 2 in force 1/1/95). Modify CE marking procedures and now include lifts for people.

Authorities   (1)   Health and Safety Executive

Trans Frontier Shipment of Waste Regulations 1994
SI 1994/1137

Commencement: 6th May 1994

Apply to England, Wales, and Scotland.

Made under the European Communities Act 1972.

Amend SI 1980/1709, SI 1991/1624, SI 1994/1056, SR 1981/252. Revokes SI 1988/1562, SI 1988/1790, SR 1989/115.

Designate authorities which are competent authorities as waste regulation authorities under Section 30 of the Environmental Protection Act 1990. They deal with notifications, financial guarantees or insurance, insurance of return and /or disposal of waste. They confer power on customs officials to detain shipments and provide for penalties for contravention

Urban Waste Water Treatment (England and Wales) Regulations 1994
SI 1994/2841

Commencement: 30th November 1994

Apply to England and Wales.

Made under the European Communities Act 1972.

Concerned with the control of pollution by incorrect disposal of waste water. Sewage undertakers must have a satisfactory collecting system, treatment plant and system, and discharge the treated waste water in a proper manner. They must monitor operations and keep records. Apply also to dumping of sludge from ships.

Urban Waste Water Treatment (Scotland) Regulations 1994
SI 1994/2842 (S144)

Commencement: 30th November 1994

Apply to Scotland.

Made under the European Communities Act 1972.

Implement DIR 91/271 in Scotland. They are concerned with the control of pollution caused by the incorrect disposal of waste water. Sewage undertakers must have a satisfactory collecting system, treatment plant system, and discharge the treated waste water in a proper manner. They must monitor operations and keep records. They also apply to the dumping of sludge from ships.

Utilities Supply and Works Contracts Regulations 1992
SI 1992/3279

Commencement: 13th January 1993

Apply England, Wales and Scotland.

Made under the European Communities Act 1972.

Amend SI 1991/2680 Public Works Contracts Regulations 1991 and are themselves amended by SI 1993/3227 Utilities Supply and Works Contracts (Amendments) Regulations 1994, which came into force on 13th January 1994.

These Regulations implement in its entirety EC Directive 90/531/EEC concerning the coordination of procedures for the award of supply and works contracts by certain entities operating in the water, energy, transport and telecommunications sectors.

Washing Facilities Regulations 1964
SI 1964/965

Commencement: 1st January 1965

Apply to England, Wales, and Scotland.

Made under the Offices, Shops, and Railway Premises Act 1963.

In premises where the above Act applies there should be provided suitable and sufficient washing facilities. These are defined by these Regulations.

Waste Management Licensing Regulations 1994
SI 1994/1056

Commencement: 1st May 1994

Apply to England, Wales and Scotland.

Made under various Acts.

Modify various Acts and SI 1985/1699, SI 1988/819, SI 1991/1624, SI 1992/588.

List exemptions from the requirements to hold a waste management licence for storing, treating and disposing of waste. Those exempt from the scheme must still register with the waste regulation authority.

Water Bye-laws 1986

Commencement: 1st January 1989

Apply to England, Wales, Scotland and Northern Ireland.

These were previously known as the Model Water Bye-laws but now have the force of law. Local water authority byelaws cannot conflict with these laws.

Authorities   (1)   Local Water Authority

                    (2)   For advice: Water Research Centre, Water Bye-laws Advisory Service. Tel No. 01495 248454

Cited Standards etc

See 'Water Supply Bye-laws Guide' Water Research Centre, Ellis Horwood, 1989.

Wireless Telegraphy (Control of Interference from Handheld Appliances, Portable Tools, etc.) (Amendment) Regulations 1985
SI 1985/808

Commencement: 29th July 1985

Apply to England, Wales, and Scotland.

Only in force until the Electromagnetic Compatibility Regulations 1992 *(Page 59)*, come fully into force (1/1/96).

Cited Standards etc

BS 800: 1988 Specification for limits and methods of measurement of radio interference characteristics of household electrical appliances, portable tools and similar electrical apparatus.

Wireless Telegraphy (Control of Interference from Ignition Apparatus) Regulations 1973
SI 1973/1217

Commencement: 1st October 1973

Apply to England, Wales, and Scotland.

Made under the Wireless Telegraphy Act 1967.

After 1st January 1996 the Electromagnetic Compatibility Regulations 1992 *(Page 59)* replace this regulation.

Wireless Telegraphy (Interference from Citizens' Band Radio) Regulations 1982
S1 1982/635

Commencement: 10th June 1982

Apply to England, Wales, and Scotland.

No Cited Standards.

Wireless Telegraphy (Interference from Electro-mechanical Apparatus) Regulations 1963
SI 1963/189

Commencement: 3rd March 1963

Apply to England, Wales, and Scotland.

Only in force until the Electromagnetic Compatibility Regulations 1992 *(Page 59)* come fully into force (1/1/96).

No Cited Standards.

Wireless Telegraphy (Interference from Fluorescent Lighting Apparatus) (Amendment) Regulations 1985
SI 1985/807

Commencement: 29th July 1989

Apply to England, Wales, and Scotland.

These supersede the 1978 Regulations SI 1978/1268 and those in turn are superseded by the Electromagnetic Compatibility Regulations 1992 *(Page 59)* on (1/1/96).

Cited Standards etc

BS 5394: 1988 Specification for limits and methods of measurement of radio interference characteristics of fluorescent lamps and luminaires.

Wireless Telegraphy (Interference from Radio Frequency Heating Apparatus) Regulations 1971
SI 1971/1675

Commencement: 21st October 1971

Apply to England, Wales, and Scotland.

Only in force until the Electromagnetic Compatibility Regulations 1992 *(Page 59)* come fully into force (1/1/96).

Cited Standards etc

BS 4809: 1972 Specification for radio interference limits and measurements for radiofrequency heating and equipment. (Now withdrawn and replaced by BS EN 55011: 1989).

Wireless Telegraphy (Short Range Devices) (Exemption) Regulations 1993
SI 1993/1591

Commencement: 26th July 1993

Apply to England, Wales, and Scotland.

Made under the Wireless Telegraph Act 1949.

Revokes SI 1959/604, SI 1991/1523, SI 1992/484.

Exempt short range devices from need for a licence but must not cause interference. Covers various equipment such as intruder alarms, safety alarms and radio hearing aids.

Amended by SI 1994/2250 which extend the range of frequencies for some equipment and extend range of categories exempt to Radio Local Area Networks (RLANS).

Workplace (Health, Safety and Welfare) Regulations 1992
SI 1992/3004

Commencement: 1st January 1993

Apply to England, Wales, and Scotland.

Made under the Health and Safety at Work etc Act 1974.

These Regulations apply to all places of work with a few exceptions, notably means of transport and construction sites.

There are requirement, regarding working environment, safety, facilities and housekeeping.

Existing workplaces will conform from 1996.

Guidance Note

Workplace Health, Safety and Welfare, HMSO, 1992.

7   FURTHER INFORMATION

The Building Regulations - Explained and Illustrated, 10th edition, V. Powell-Smith and M. J. Billington, Blackwell Science, 1995. (Due out July 1995)

Architects Legal Handbook 6th Edition, Ed. A Speight and G Stone, Butterworth-Heinmann. (Due out in 1995).

Current Awareness

A.   Acts of Parliament

HMSO Monthly Catalogue, HMSO.

B.   Statutory Instruments

List of Statutory Instruments together with the list of Statutory Rules of Northern Ireland for the month of ...... HMSO. Published monthly.

C.   Journals

Construction Industry Law Letter, published by Legal Studies and Services (Publishers) Ltd, Ludgate House, 107 Fleet Street, London, E14 9FT. Tel: 0171 936 2019.

Construction Law Journal, published by Sweet and Maxwell Ltd, 8th Floor, South Quay Plaza, 183 Marsh Wall, London, E14 9FT. Tel: 0171 538 8686.

Constructional Law, published by Constructional Legal Press Ltd, Berkley House, 31 Bower Way, Slough, SL1 5HW. Tel: 01628 667441.

Construction Product Directive, published by the Builder Group Plc, Builder House, 1 Millharbour, London, E14 9RA. Tel: 0171 537 2222.

Construction Law, published by Eclipse Group Ltd, 18-20 Highbury Place, London, N5 1QP. Tel: 0171 354 5858.

Directories

Directory of British and Irish Law Libraries. Legal Information Resources, 1 New Road, Hebden Bridge, HX7 5DE. Tel: 01422 882895. 4th Edition, 1992.

Directory of Information Sources in the United Kingdom, Ed. Keith Reynard, ASLIB, London. 8th Edition, 1994.

European Law

SPEARHEAD - online database of existing and forthcoming European Commission Legislation. Department of Trade and Industry.

European Legislation and Standardisation, BRE, Digest No. 376. Building Research Establishment, Watford, 1992.

Commission of the European Communities, Jean Monnet House, 8 Storey's Gate, London SW1P 3AT. Tel: 0171-973-1992

BSRIA EuroCentre Publications

The Practical Guide to EC Rules for Building Services Products. BSRIA, 1995.

Framework of European Legislation and Standards. BSRIA, 1993.

European Legislation and Standard Reference Manual - handbook and subscription service (updates every 2 months). BSRIA.

Other Publications

Croner's Health and Safety at Work. Croner Publications Ltd, Kingston-upon-Thames, UK, (updated monthly).

8   SUBJECT INDEX TO ACTS AND REGULATIONS

LIST OF INDEX TERMS

©BSRIA

©BSRIA